Newspaper Girls
52 Weeks of Women
by Mike Hoffman

ISBN-13: 978-1500666286

ISBN-10: 1500666289

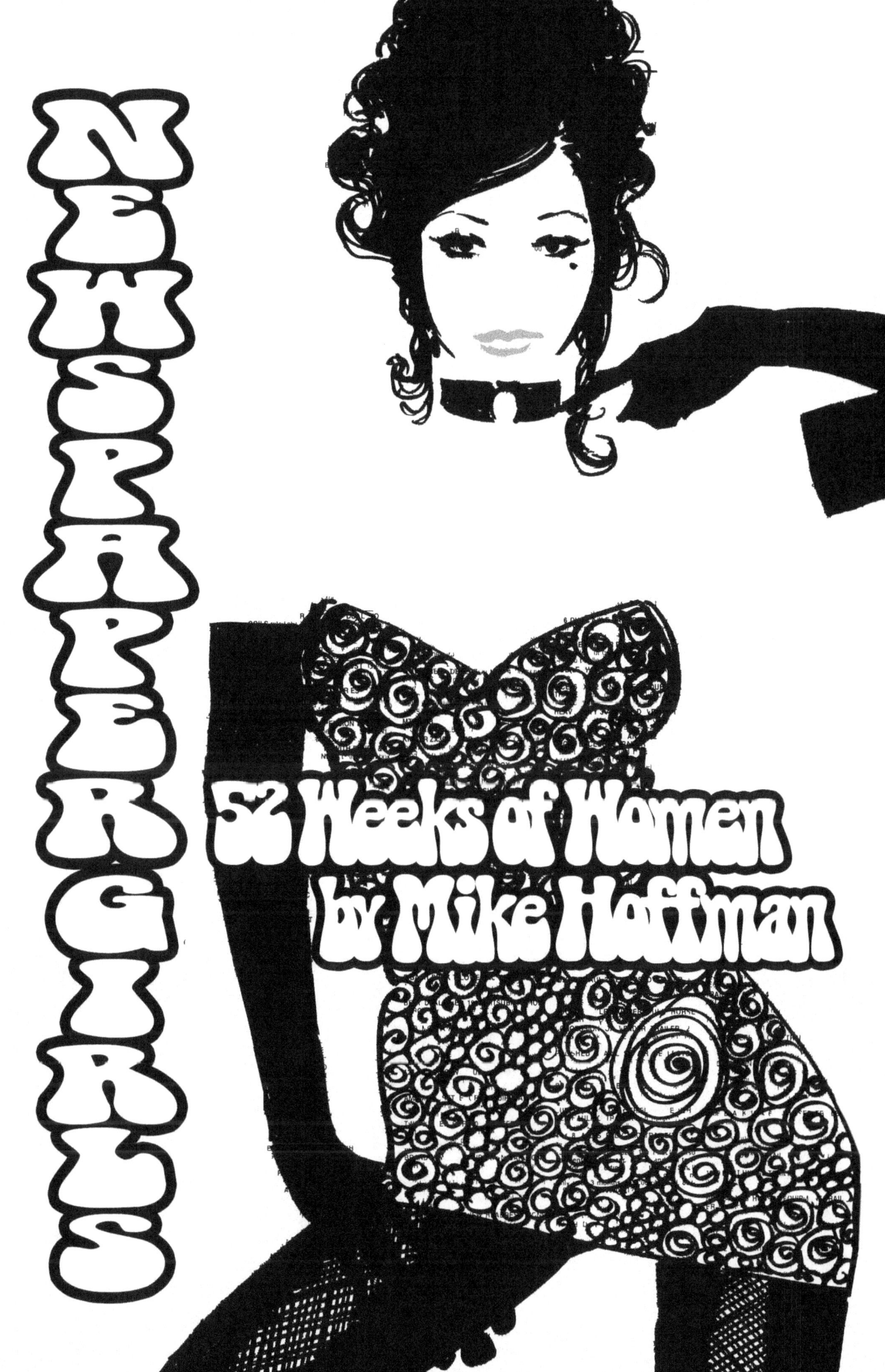

NEWSPAPER GIRLS

52 Weeks of Women
by Mike Hoffman

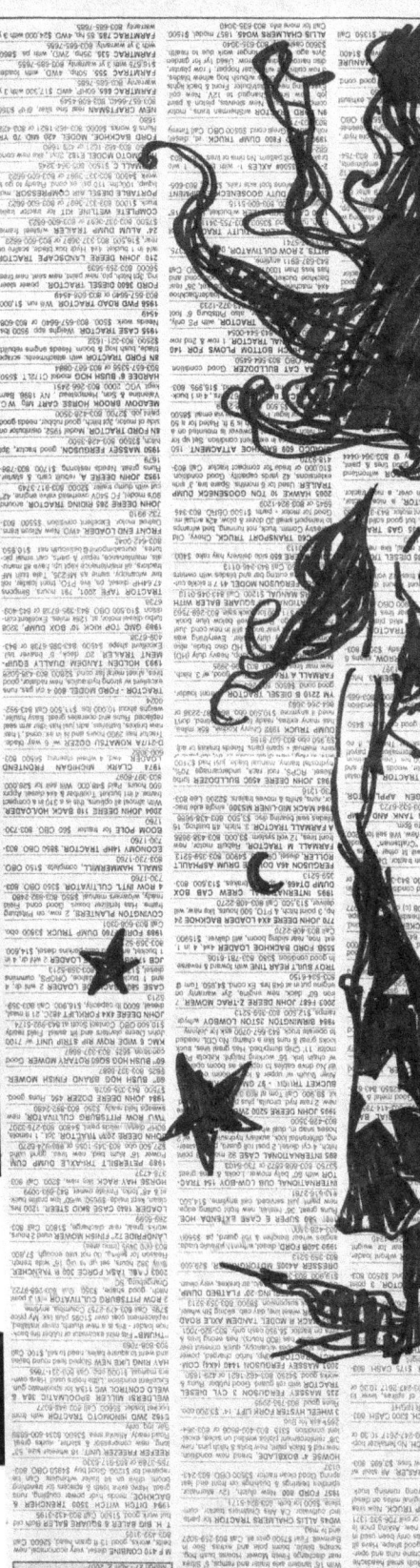

NUMBER I Humble Beginnings

NUMBER I

A Graven Error

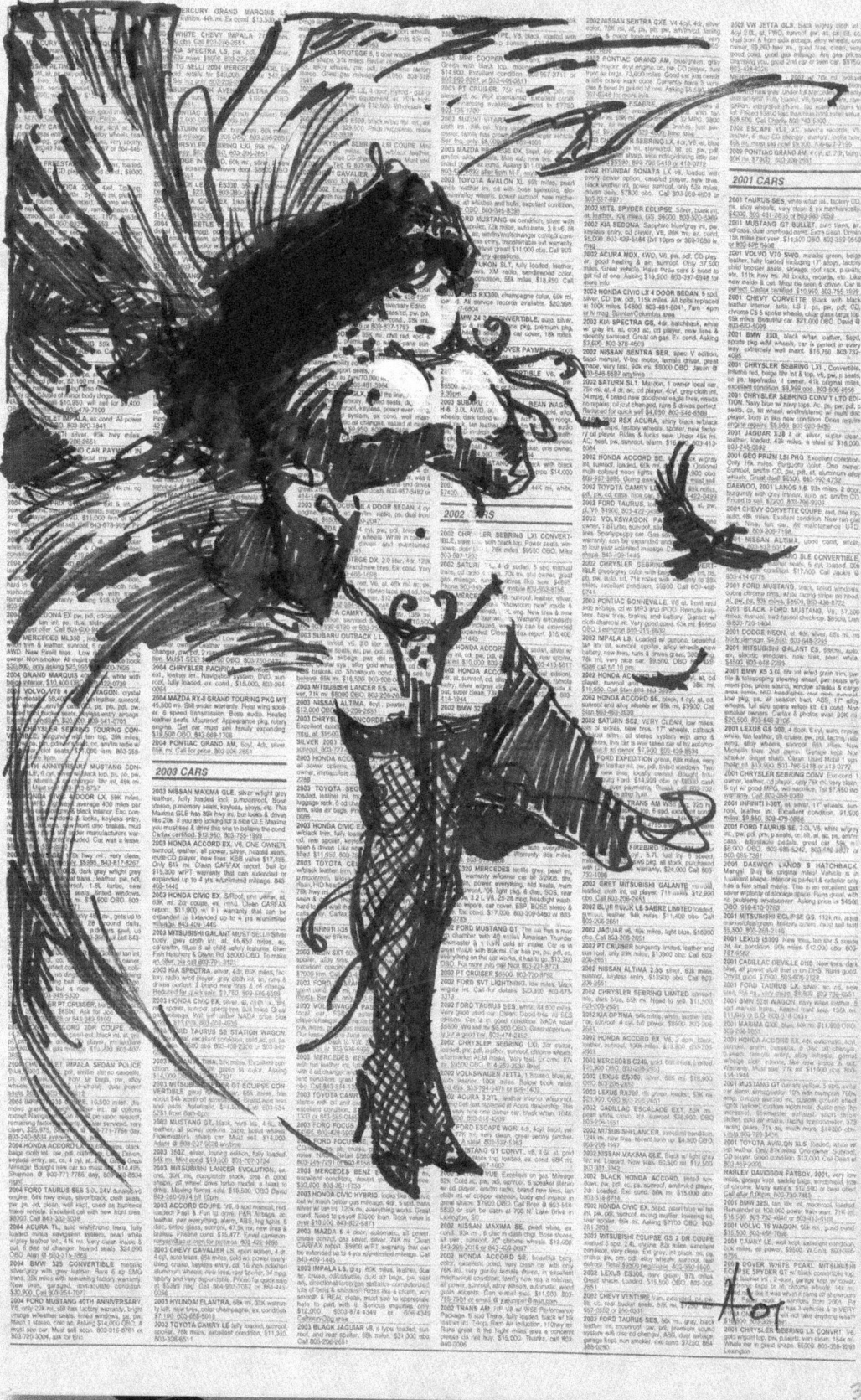

NUMBER3 All Behind Me Now

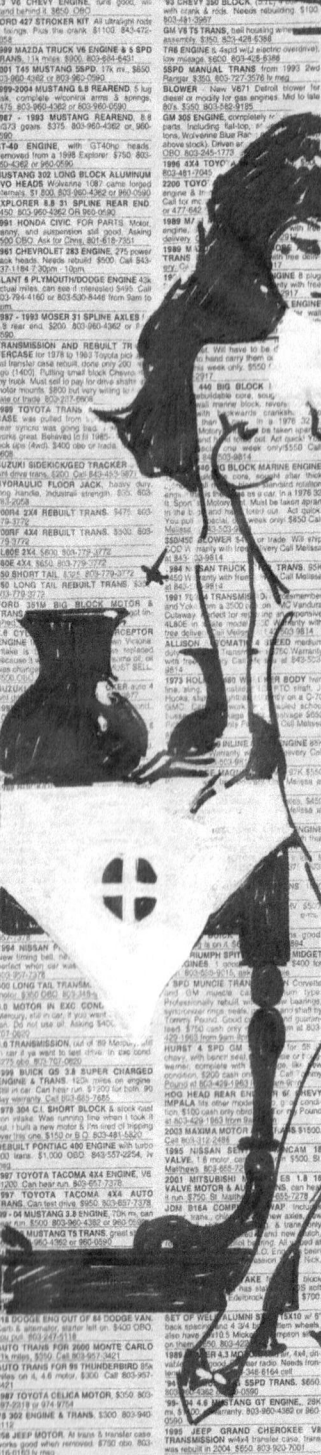
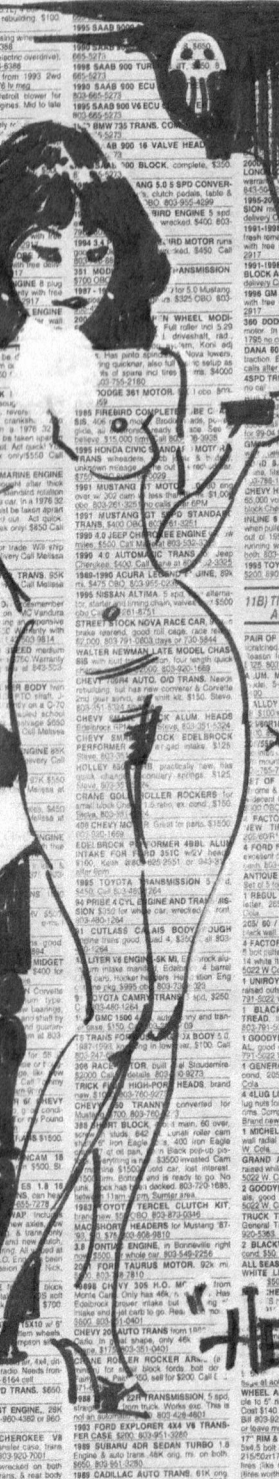
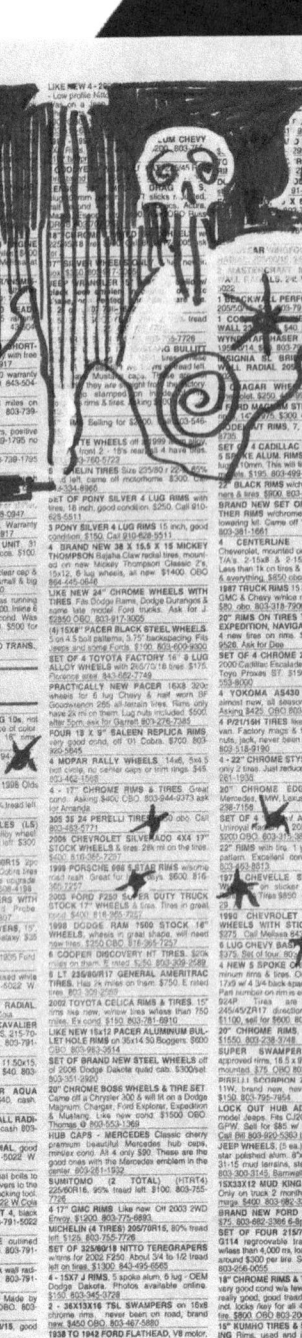

NUMBER 4 Hell Hath No Fury

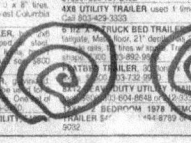
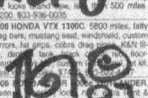

NUMBERS Hell's Hot for Sinners

NUMBER 6   What Can You Do?

NUMBER1 Bad Smoker

NUMBER 8   Paula Knows Best

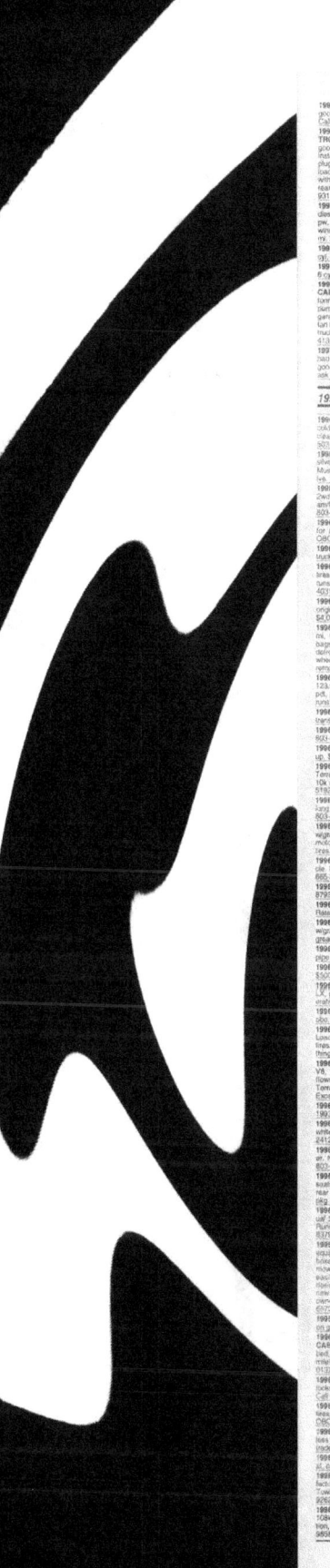

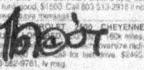

©2007 The Carolina Trader Inc.

NUMBER9   I Went Missing

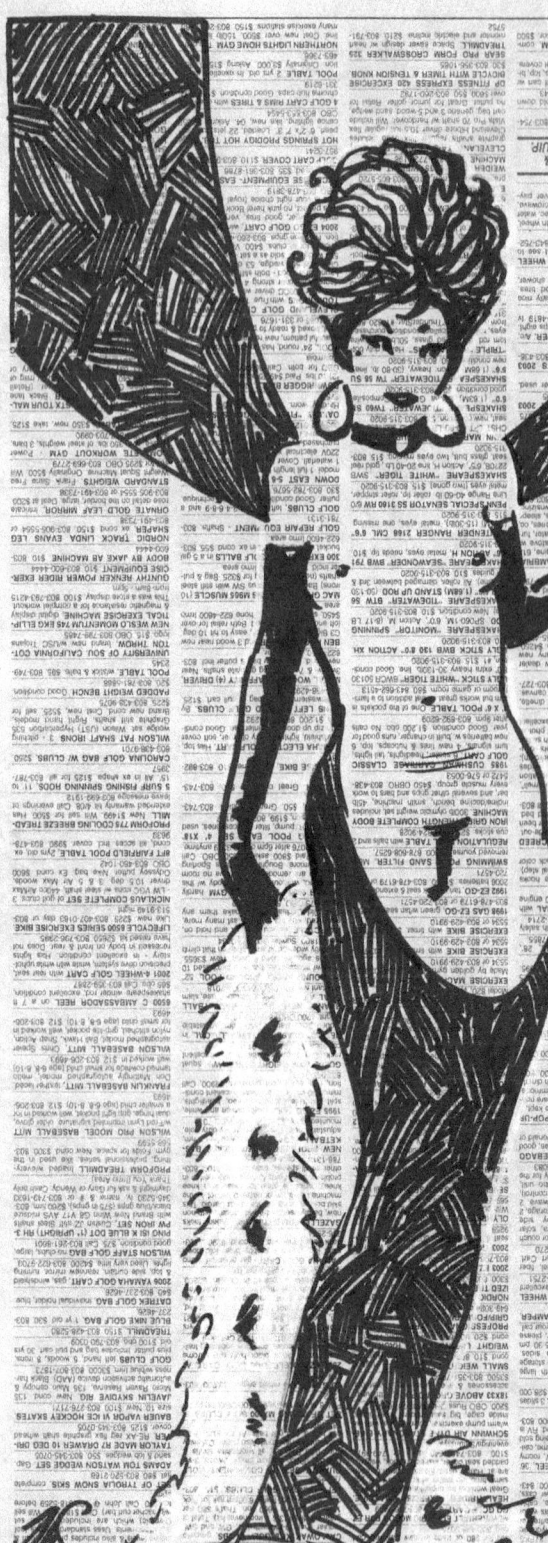

NUMBER10   Classy Actress

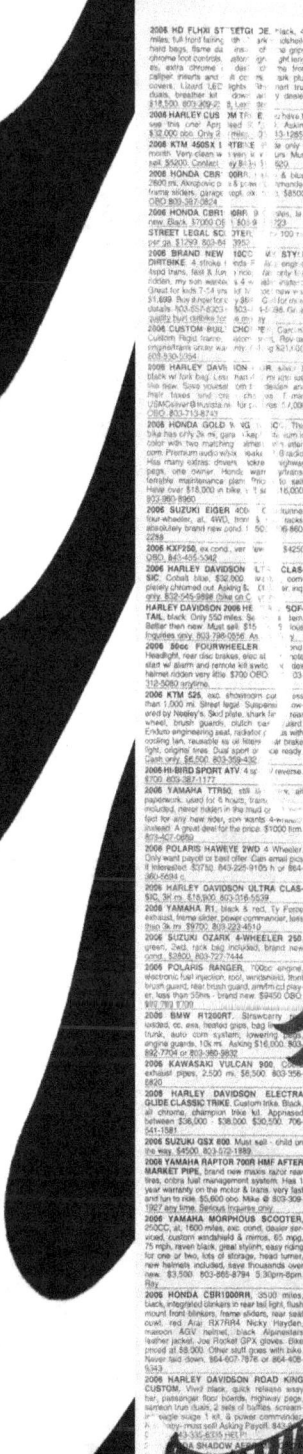

NUMBER 12   Hello Halo

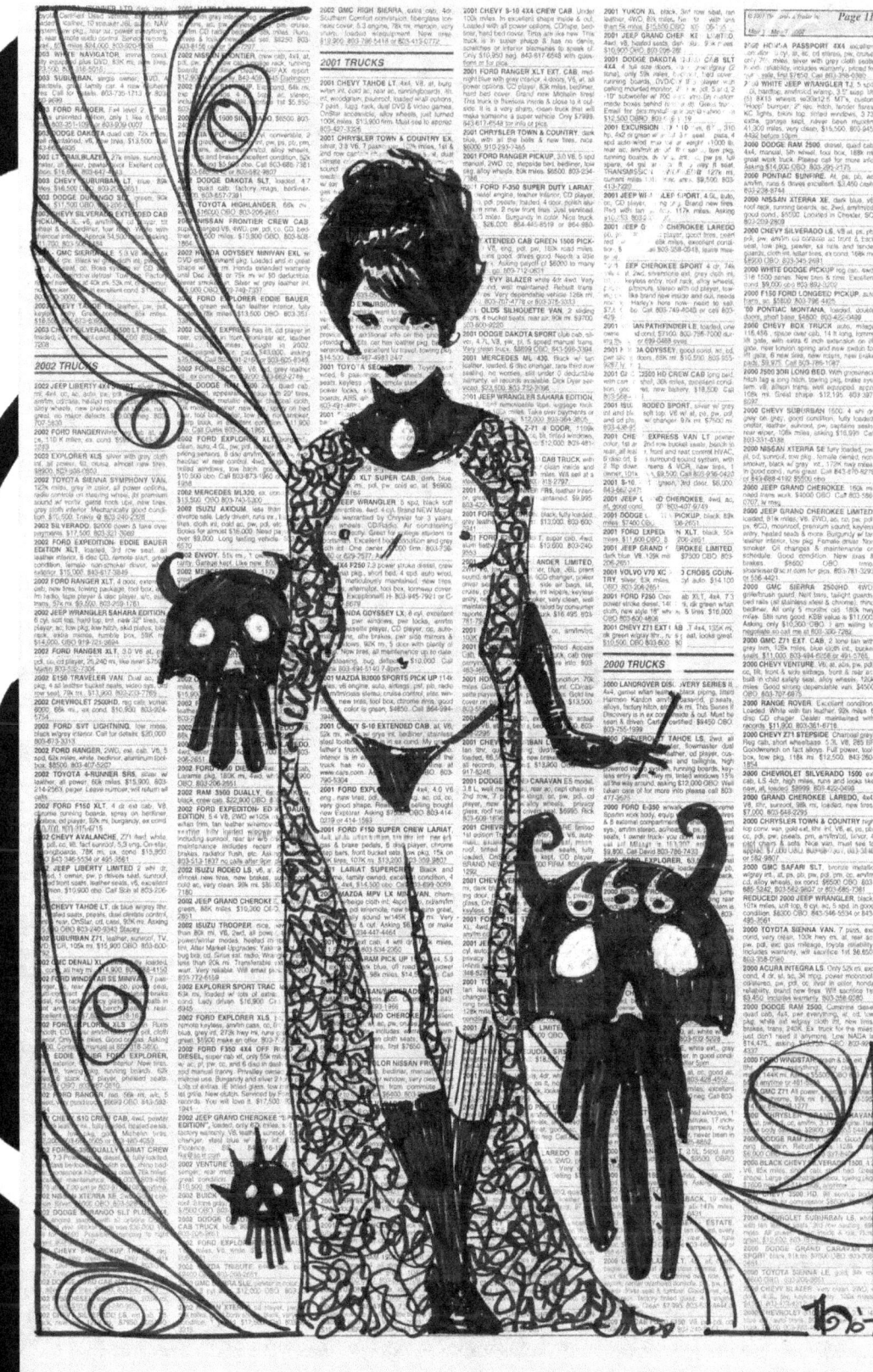

NUMBER13   Danger Delilah

NUMBER 14   Black Sheep

NUMBER 15   Summer Heat

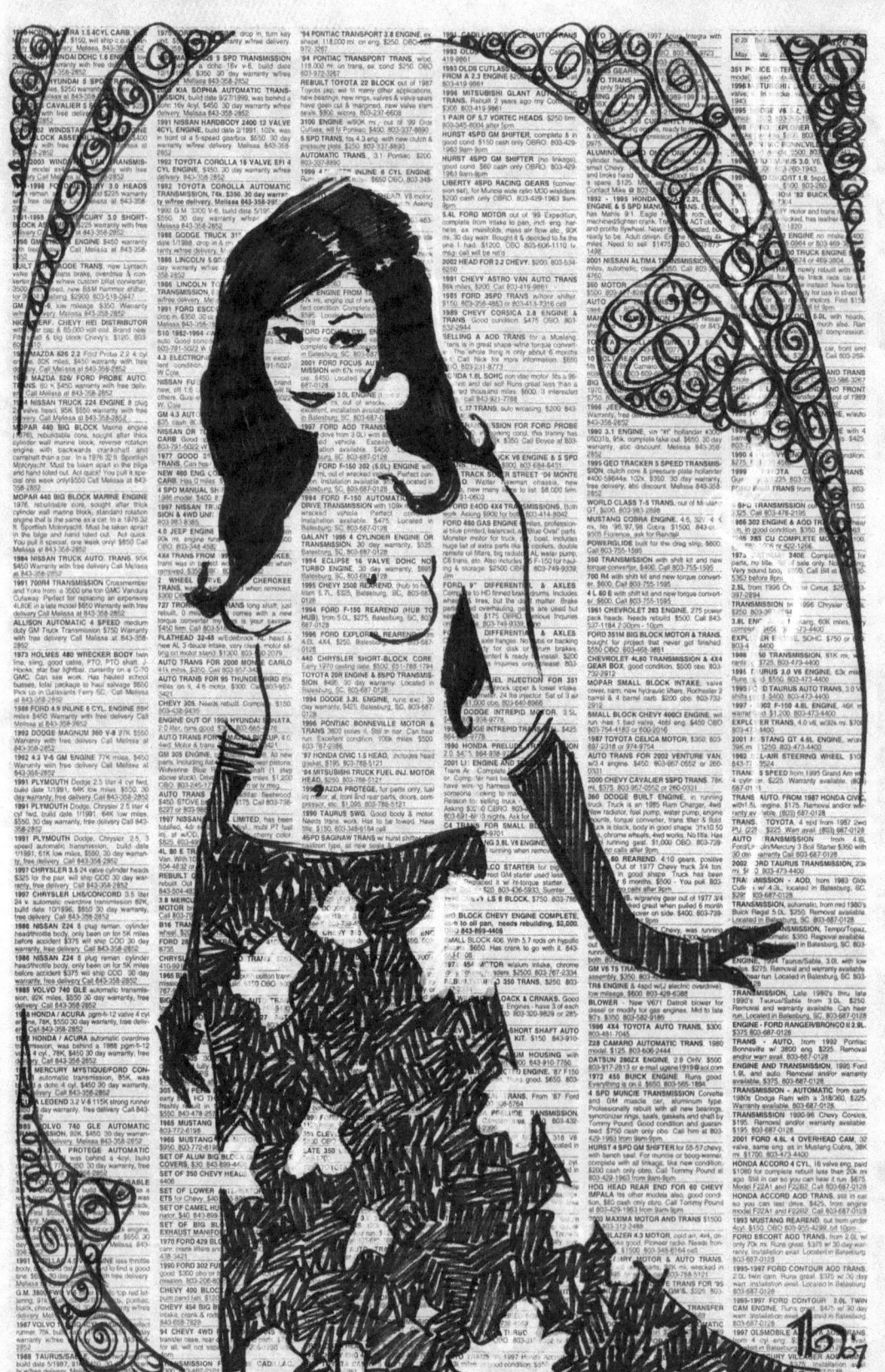

NUMBER16   Topless Tracery

NUMBER 17   Babushka Jones

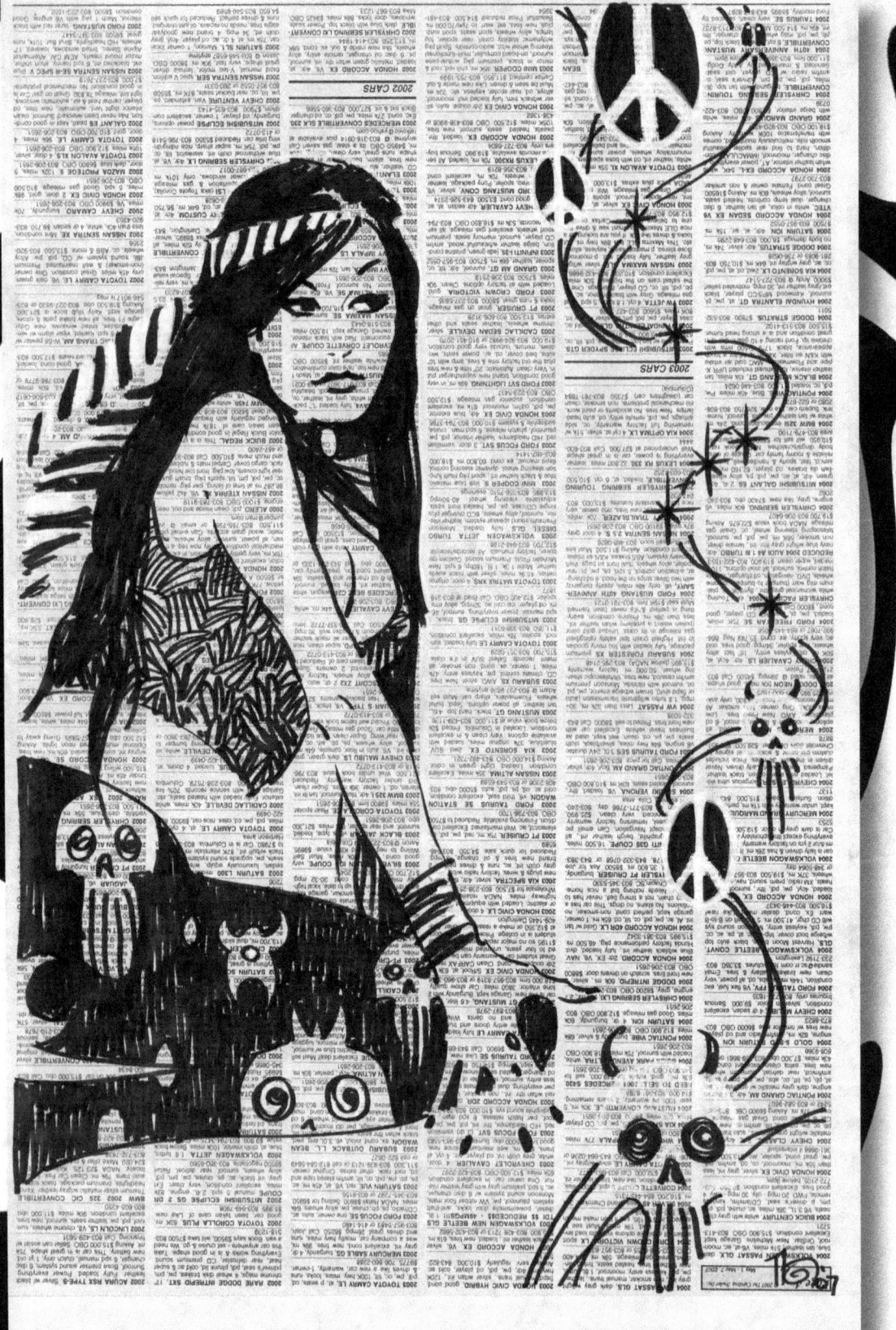

NUMBER18 **Helen of Joy**

NUMBER 19   Don't Even Write

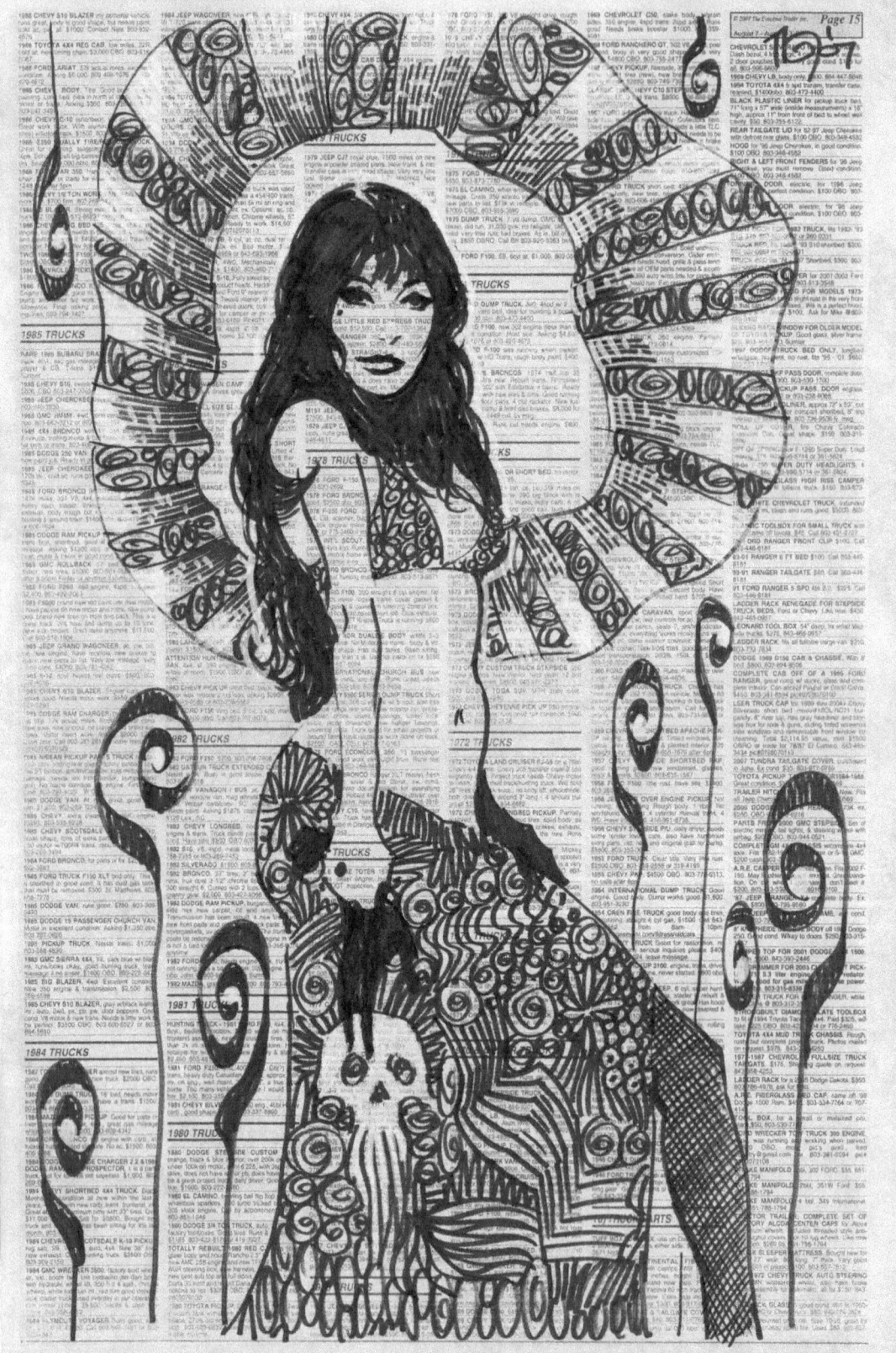

NUMBER 20   The Glove is Off

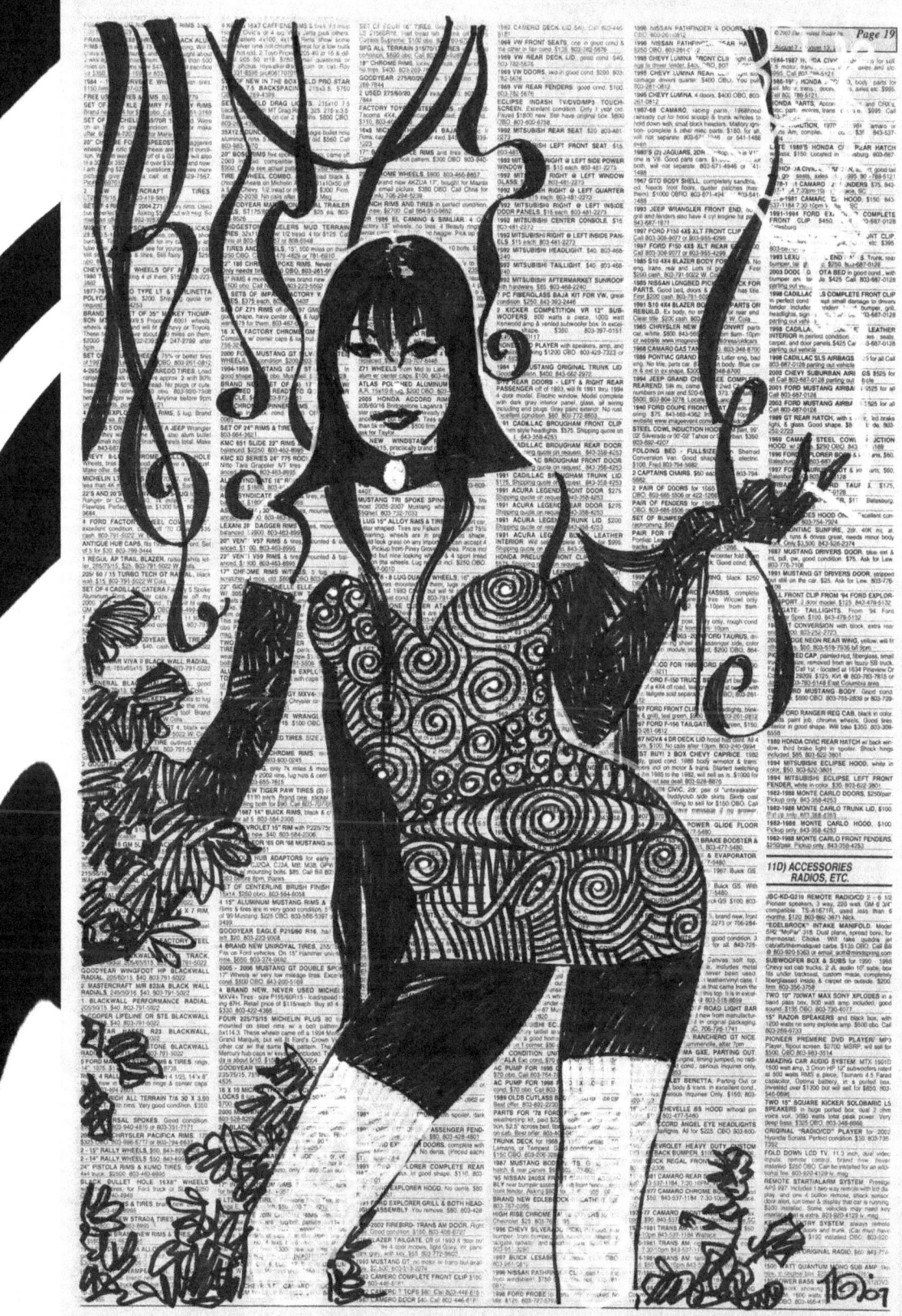

NUMBER 21 The Party Moved Outside

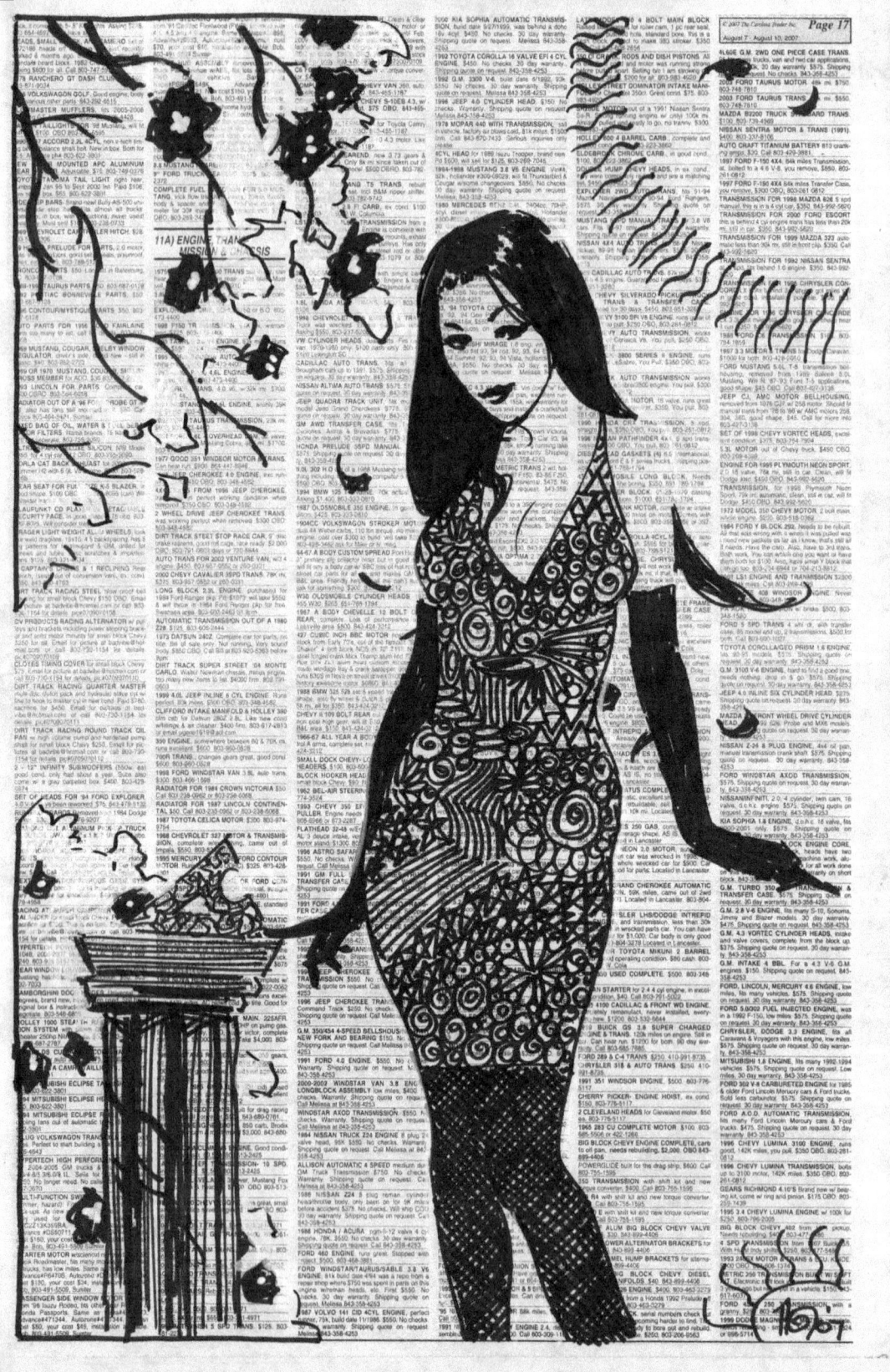

NUMBER22   Cool Sun Heat

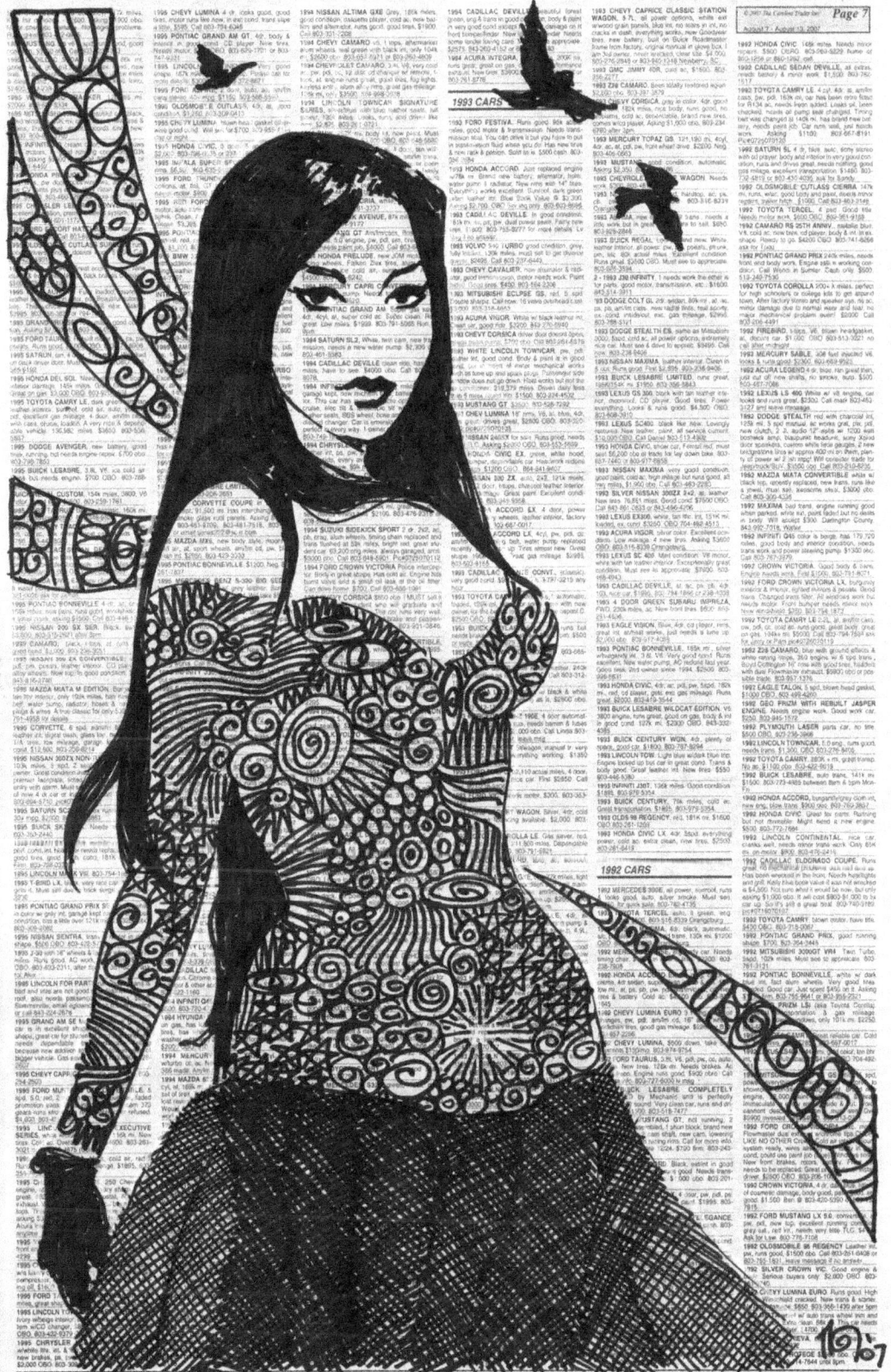

NUMBER 23 Billy Birdwatcher

NUMBER 24 That Time of Year

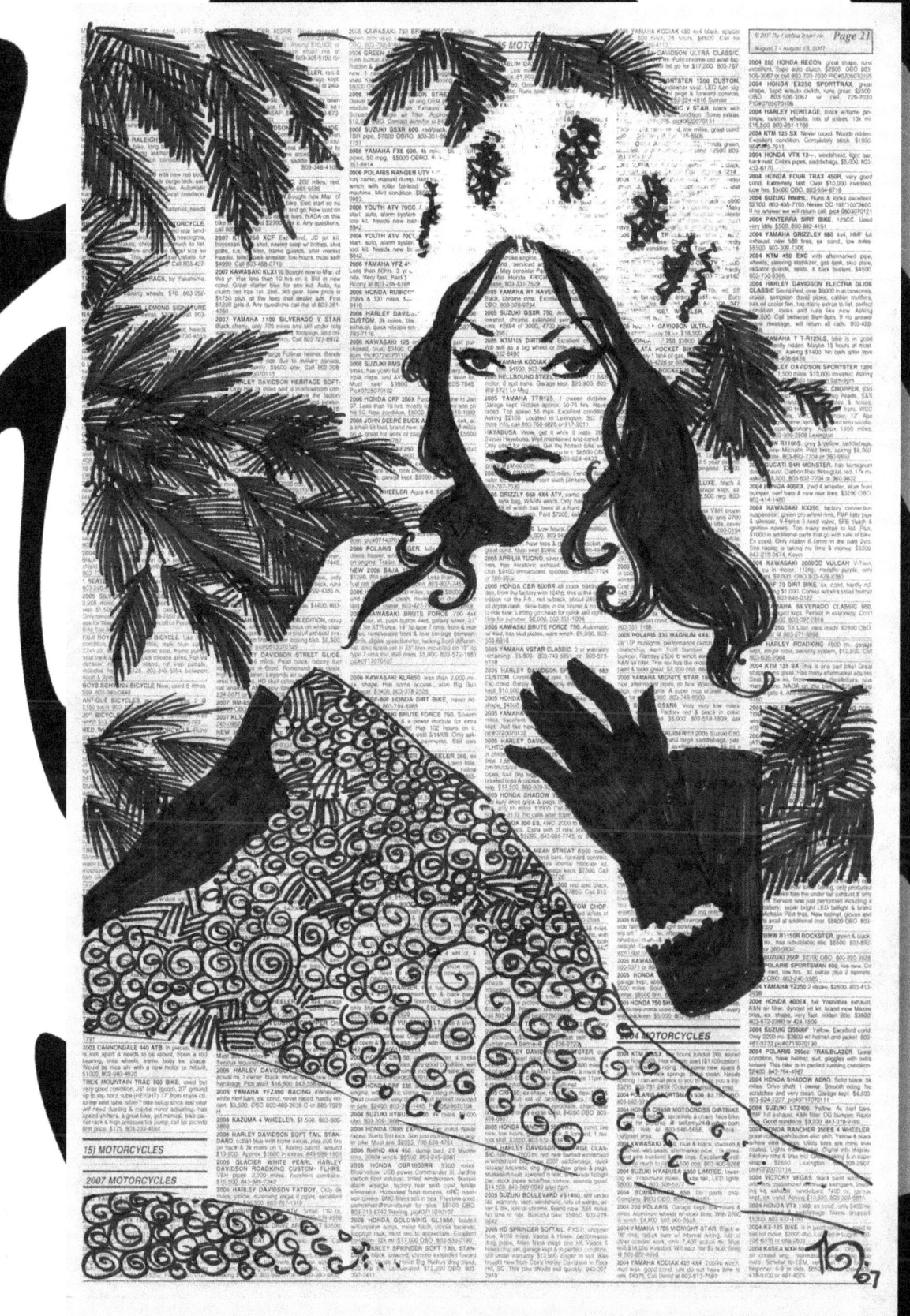

NUMBER 25 Eleanora Winters

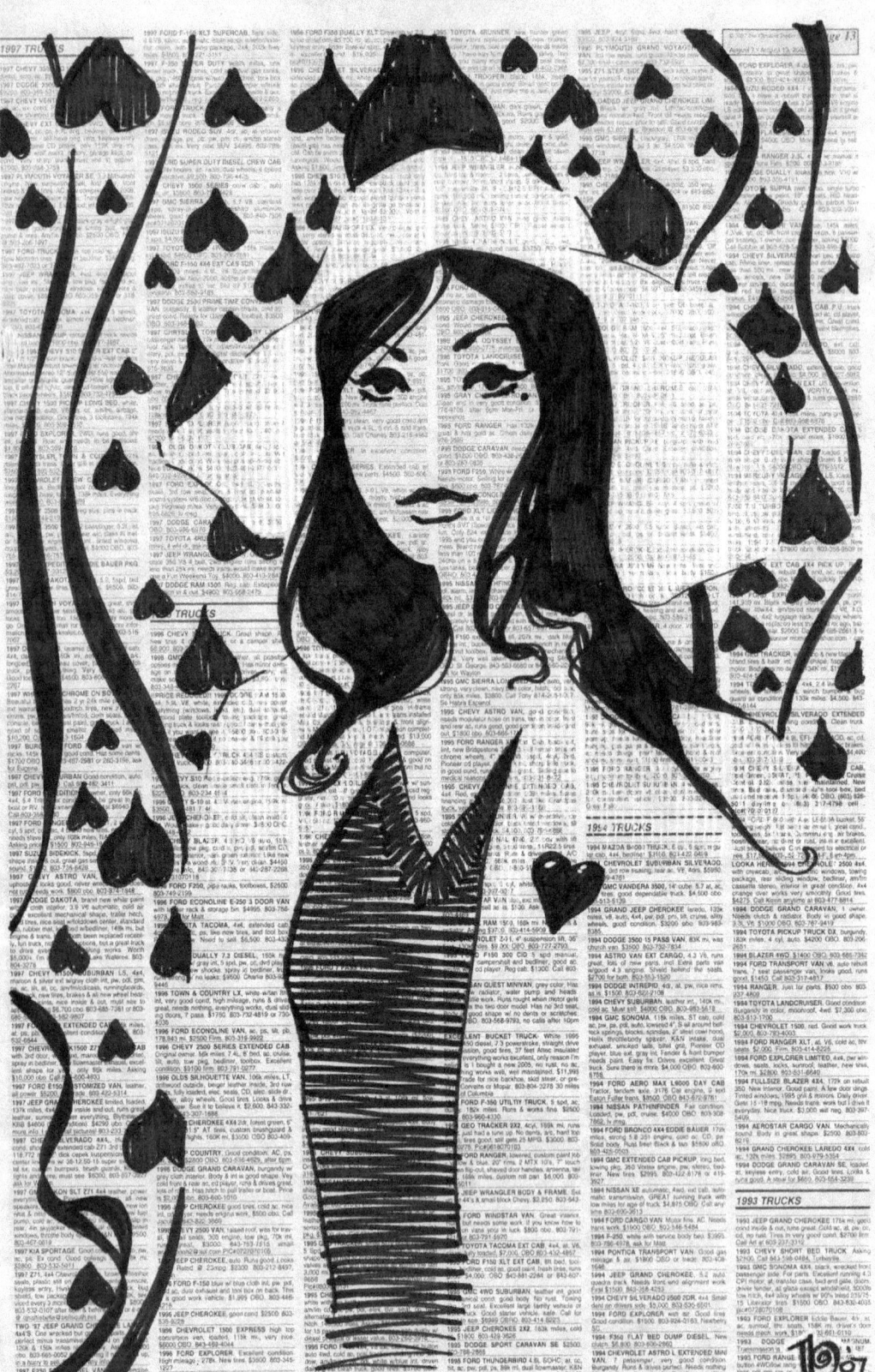

NUMBER 6 It Only Takes One

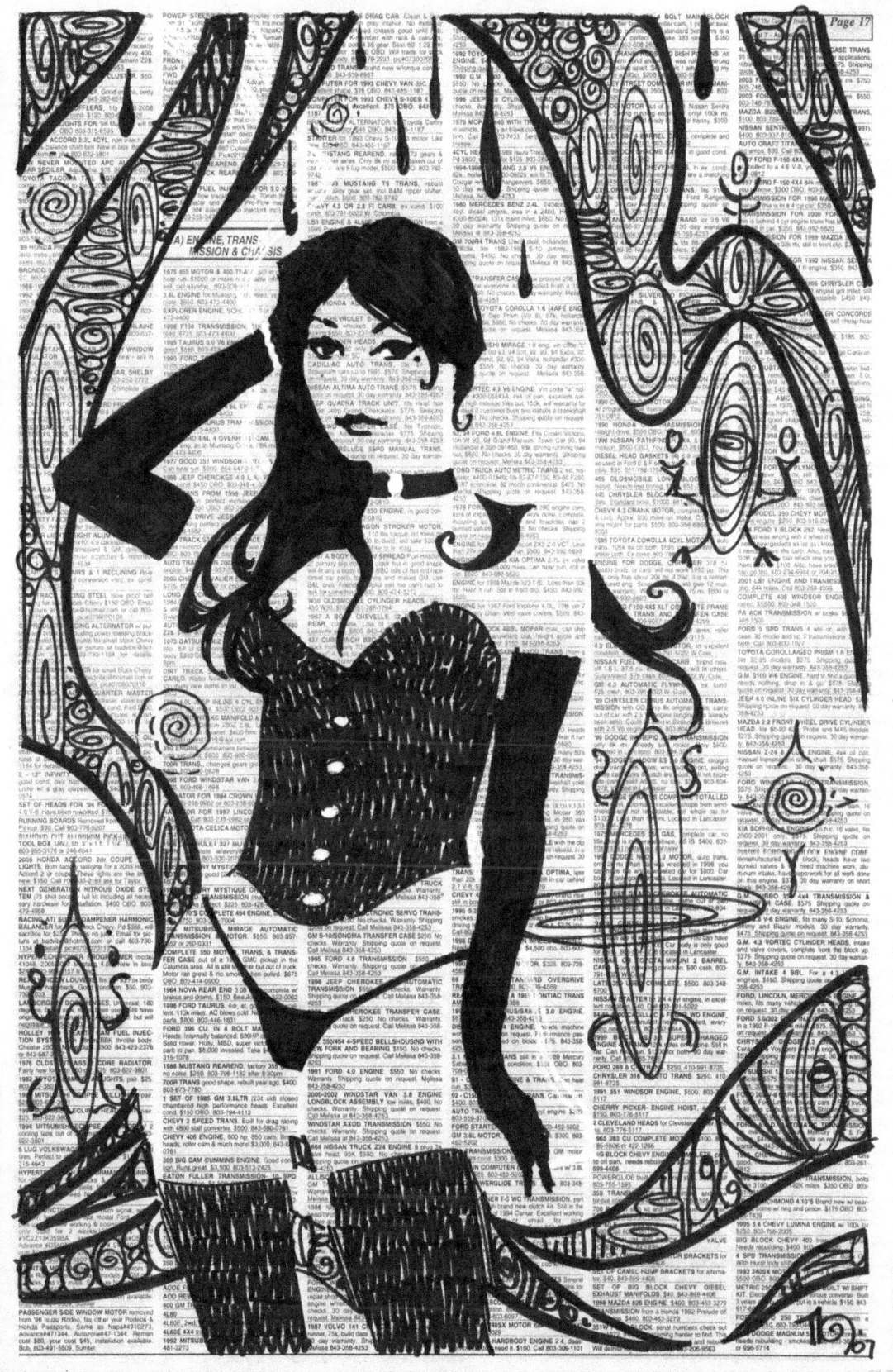

NUMBER27 You Were In My Dream

NUMBER 28 Too Much to Bare

NUMBER 29   Starry Tina

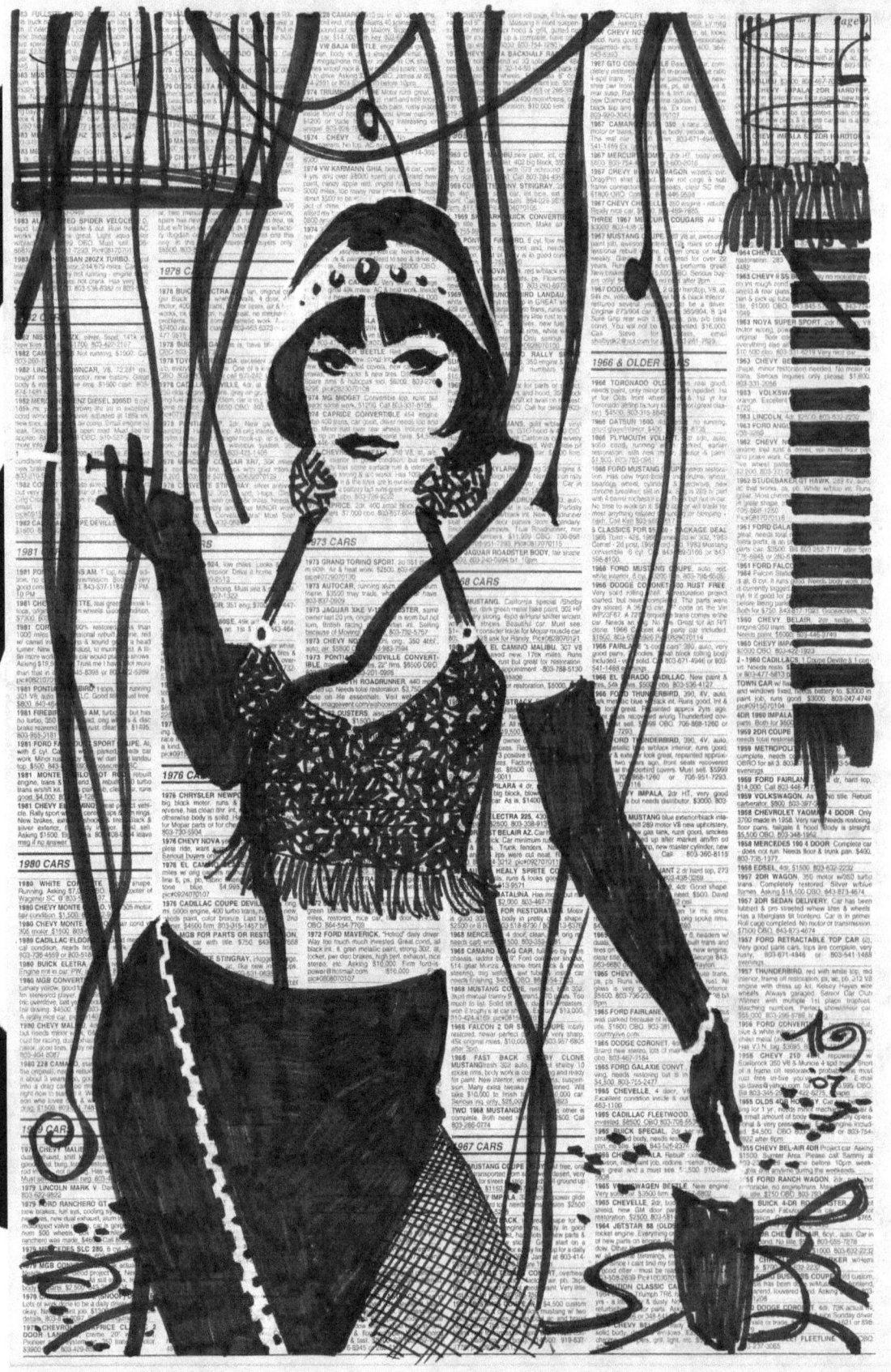

NUMBER30   Twenties Toker

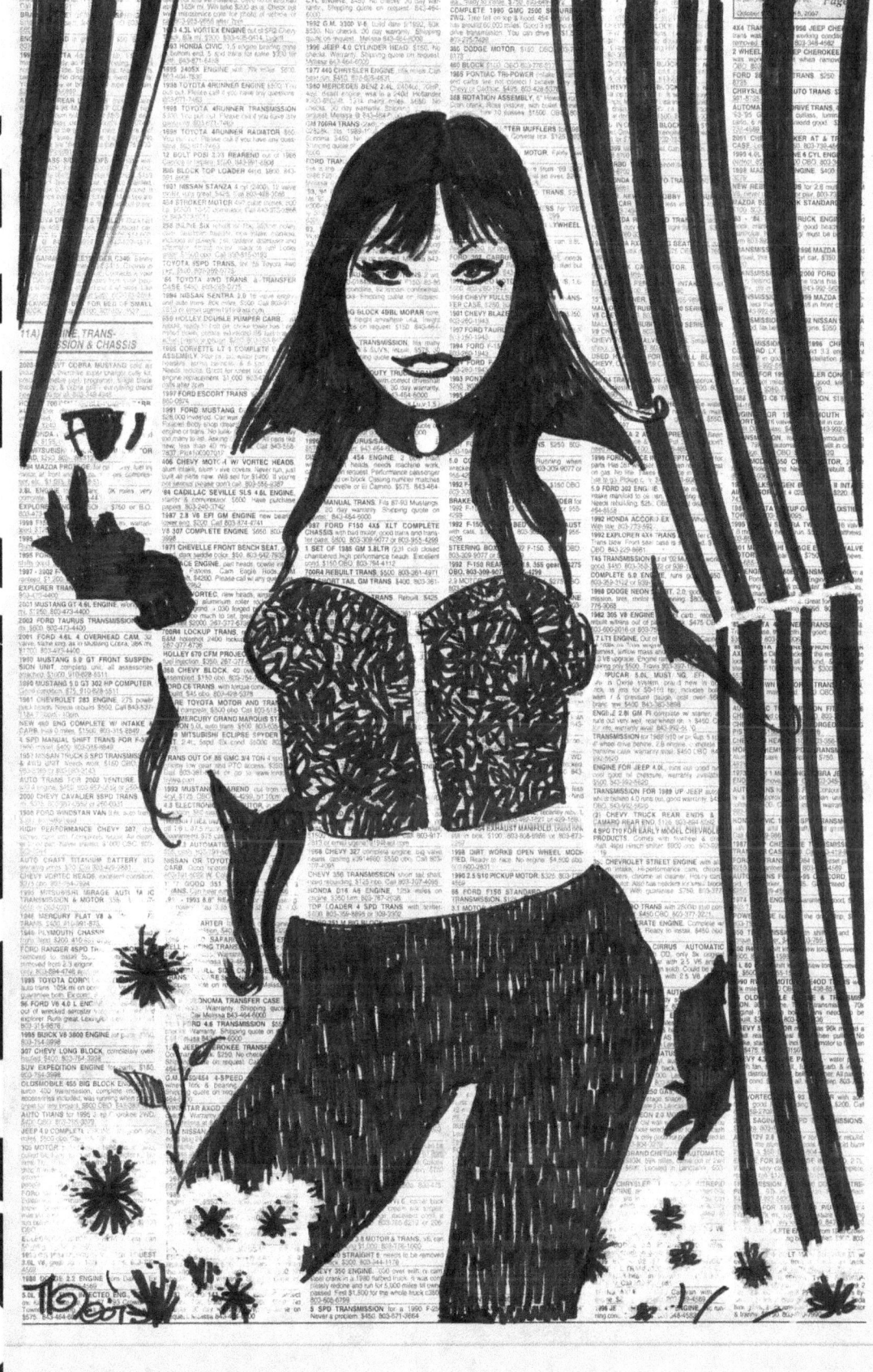

NUMBER 31   Toast of the Town

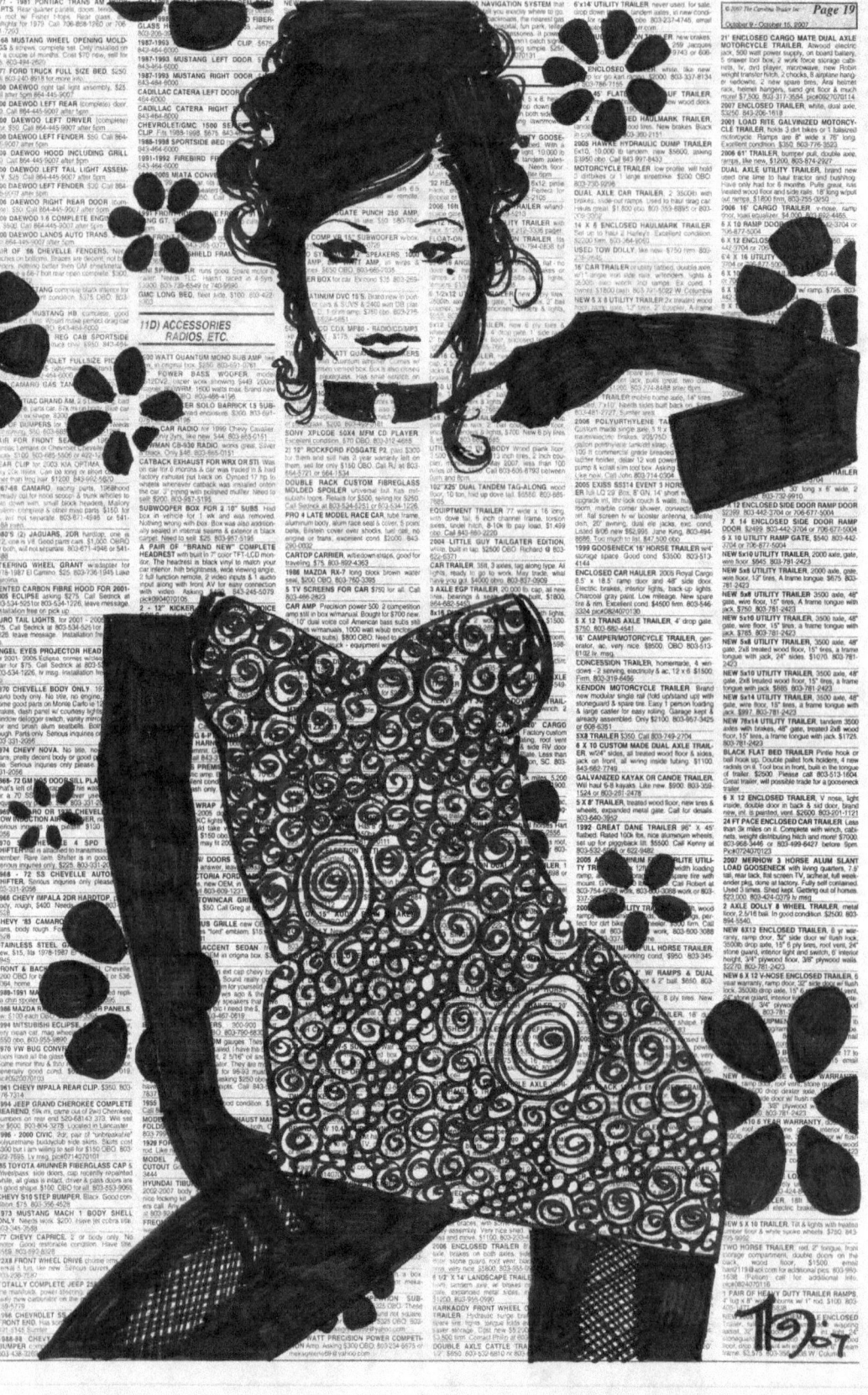

NUMBER32 Greta is Groovy

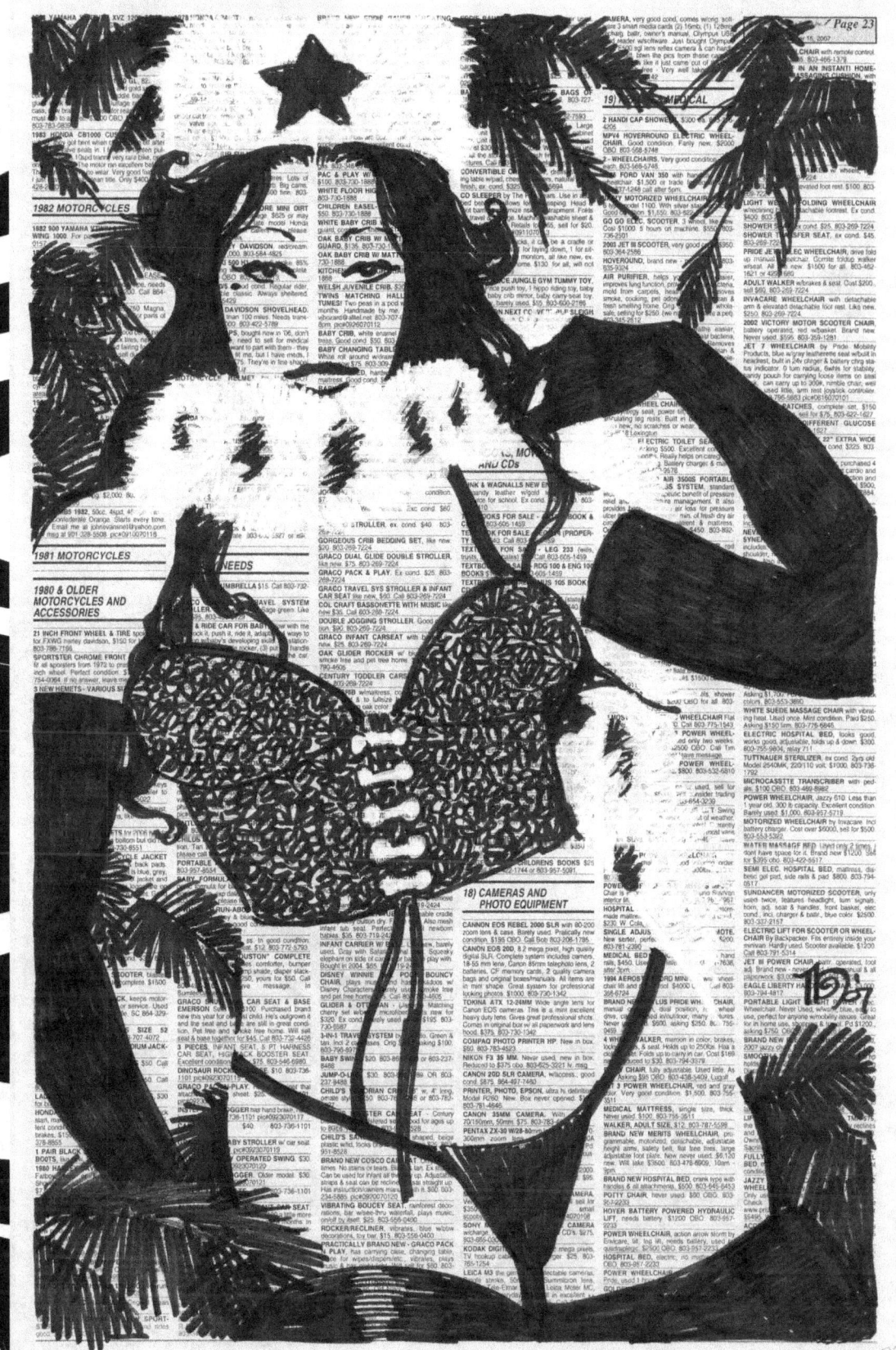

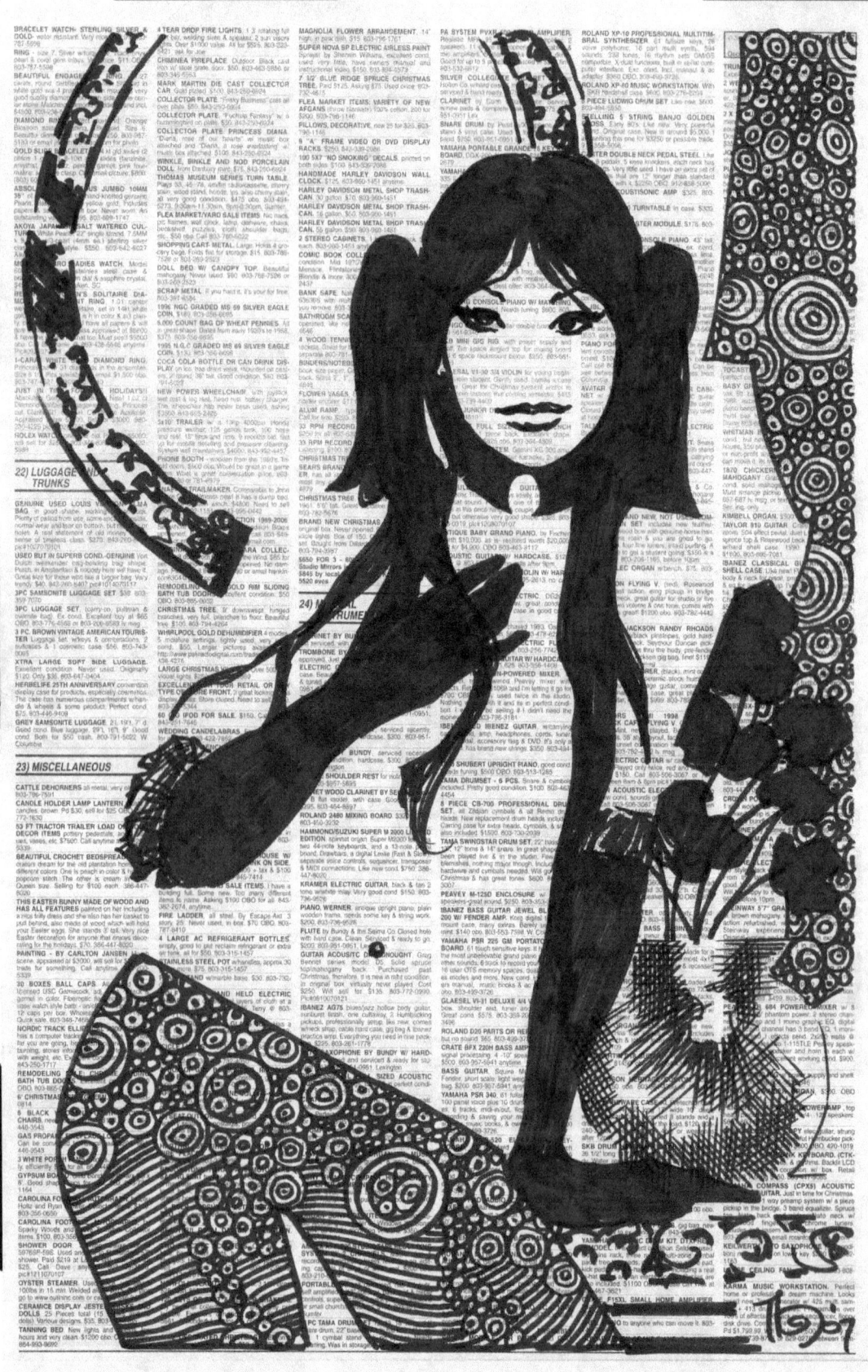

NUMBER 39 Ruby's Late Again

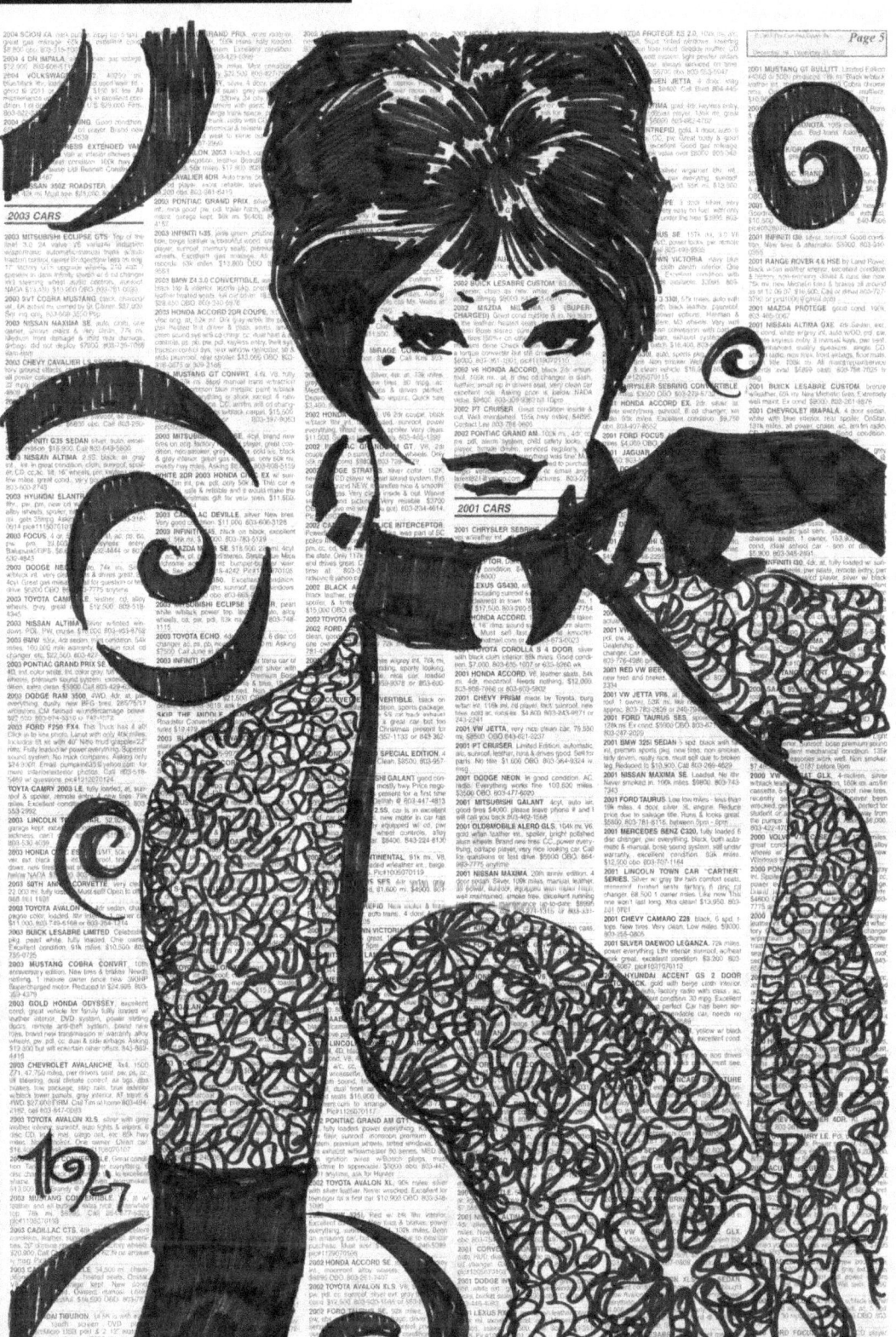

NUMBER35 The Mild Version

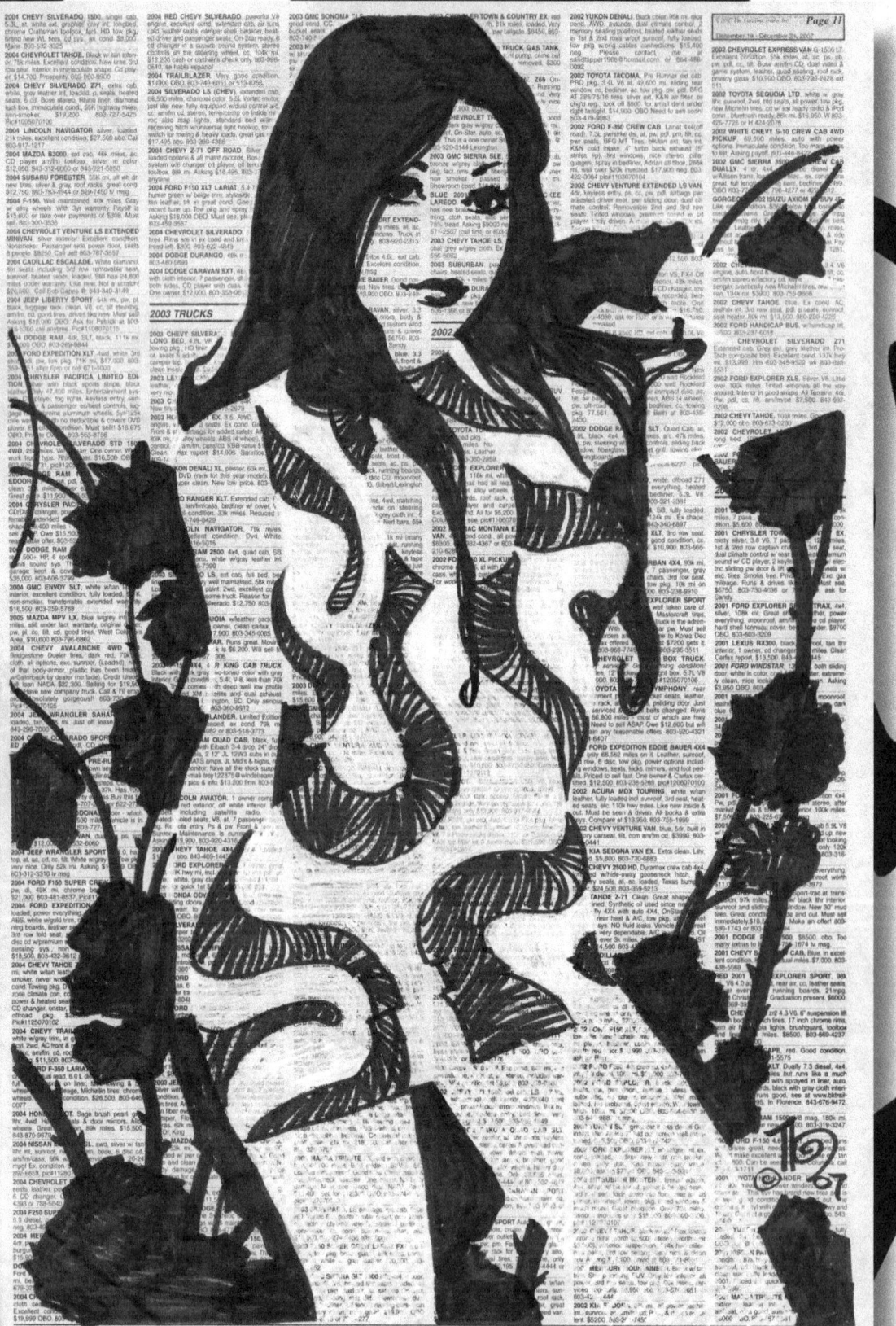

NUMBER 36 Your Rose Garden

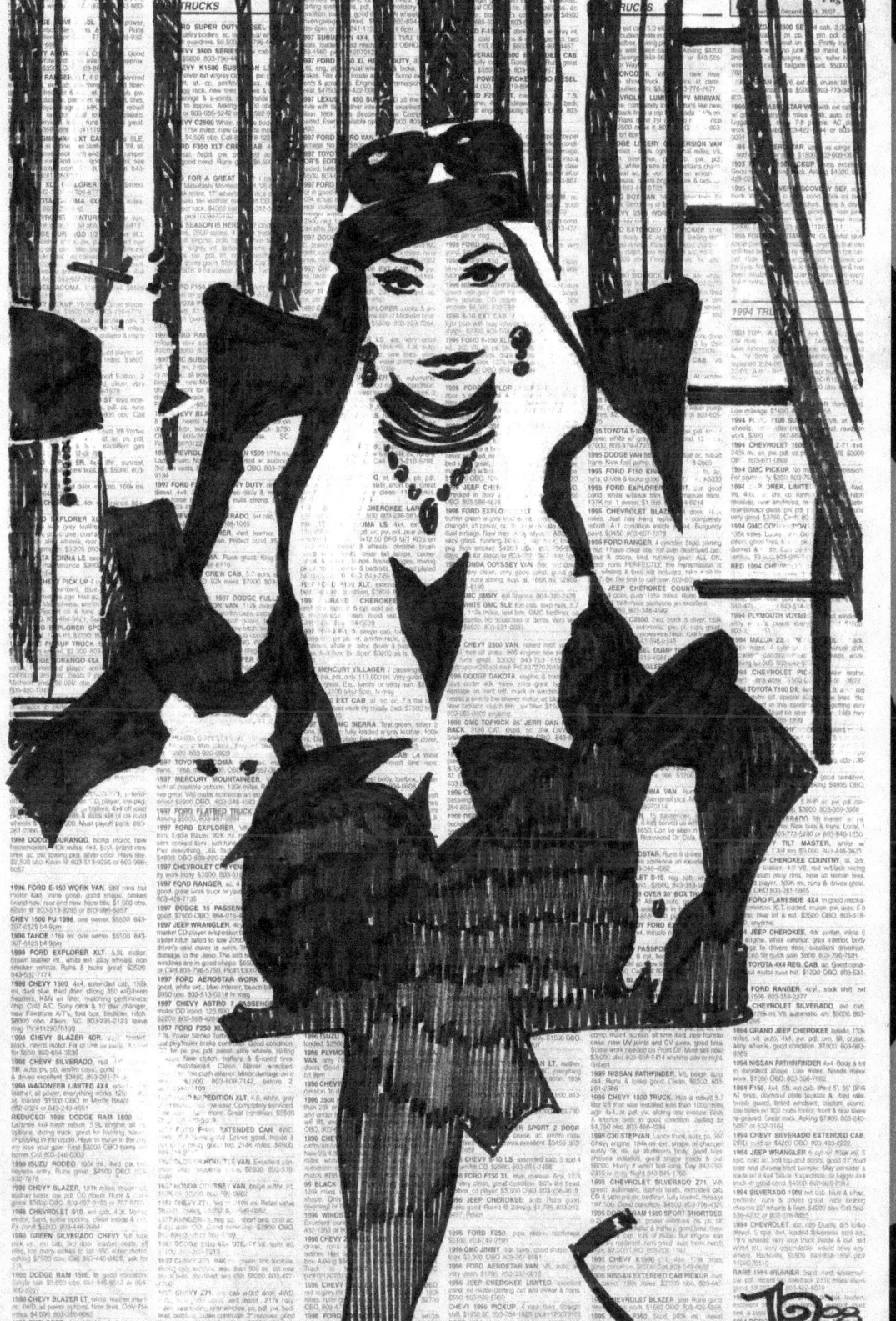

NUMBER37 3:00AM Ali's Well-Lit

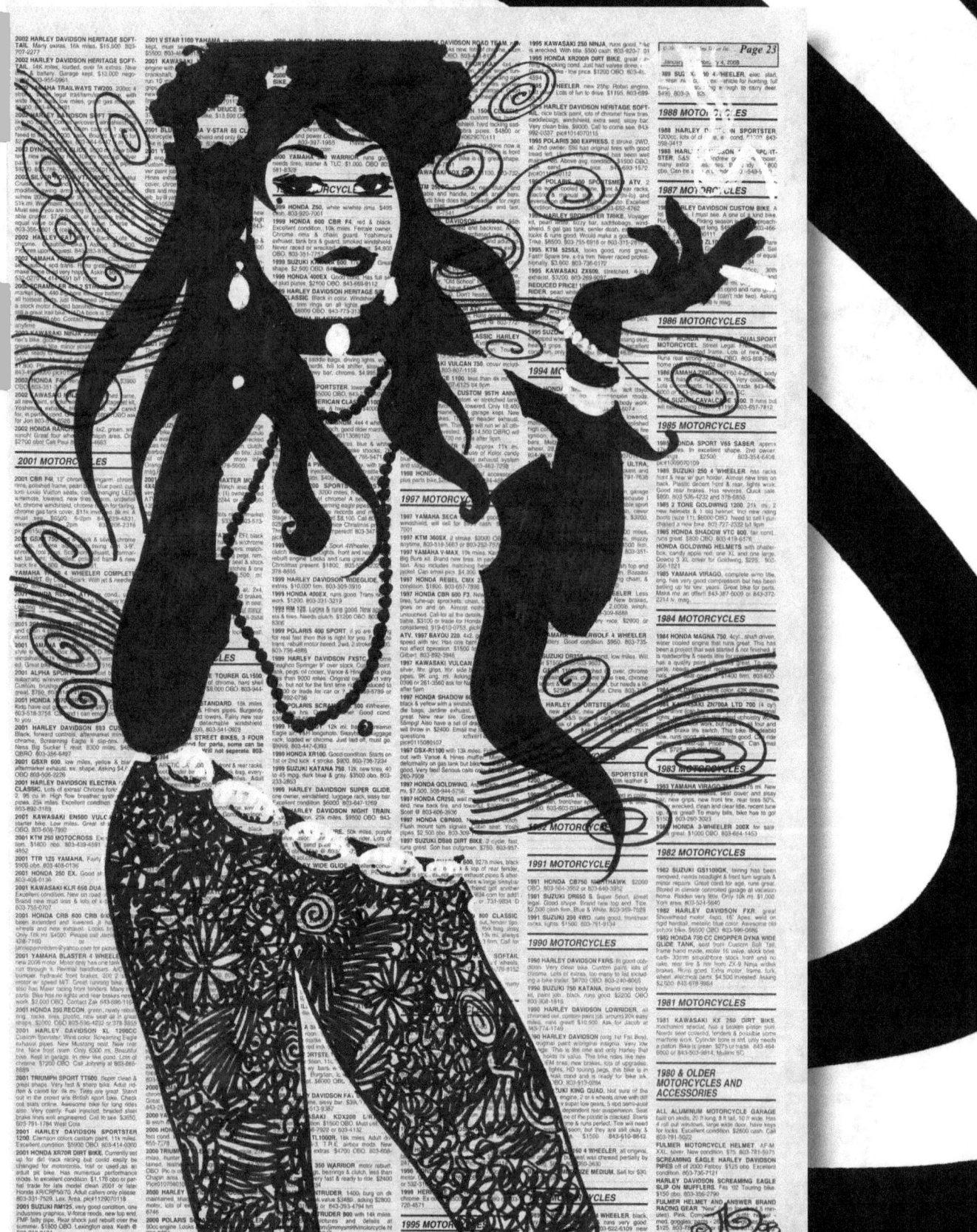

NUMBER38 Alice Told the Truth

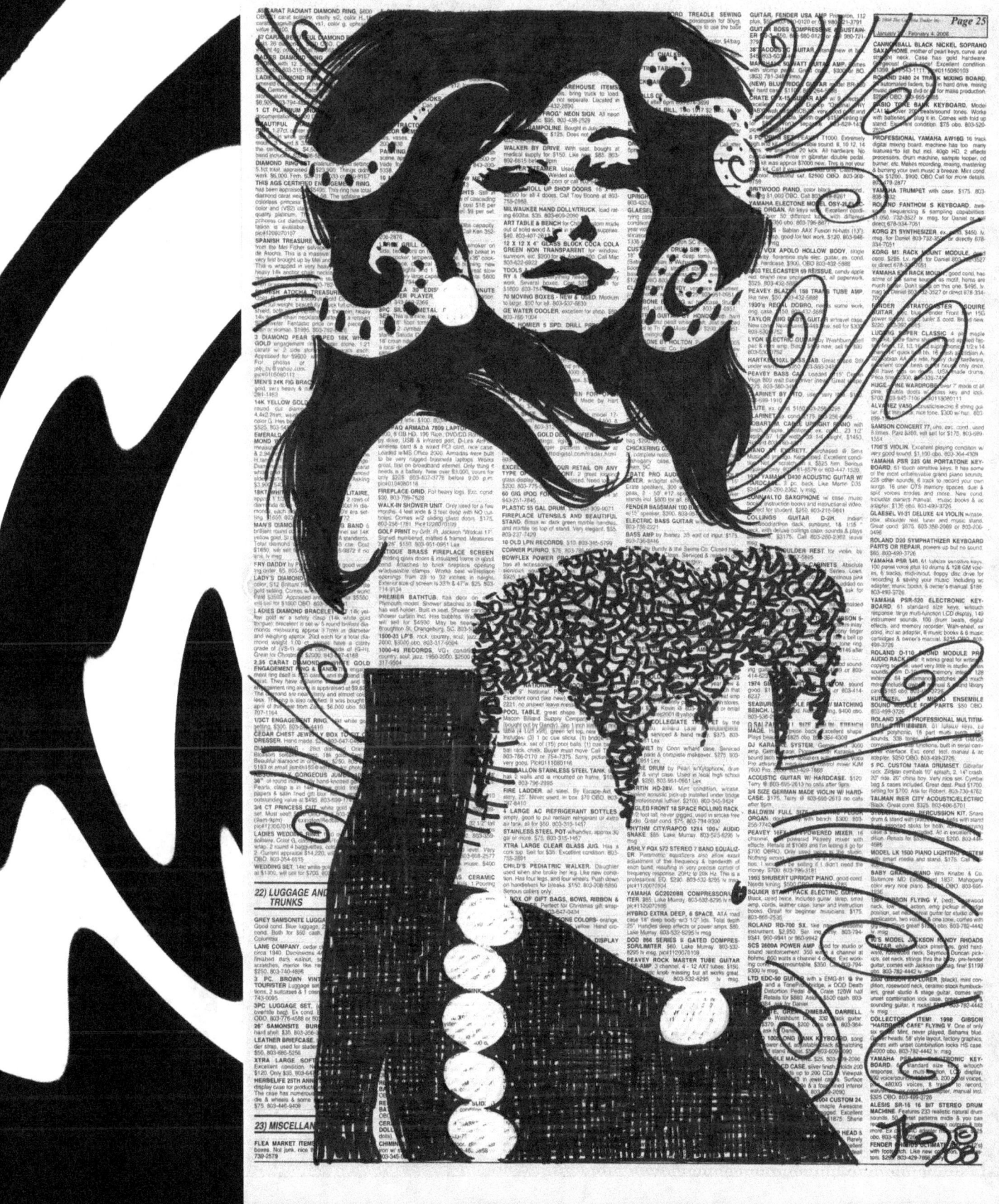

NUMBER 39 Just Like Candy

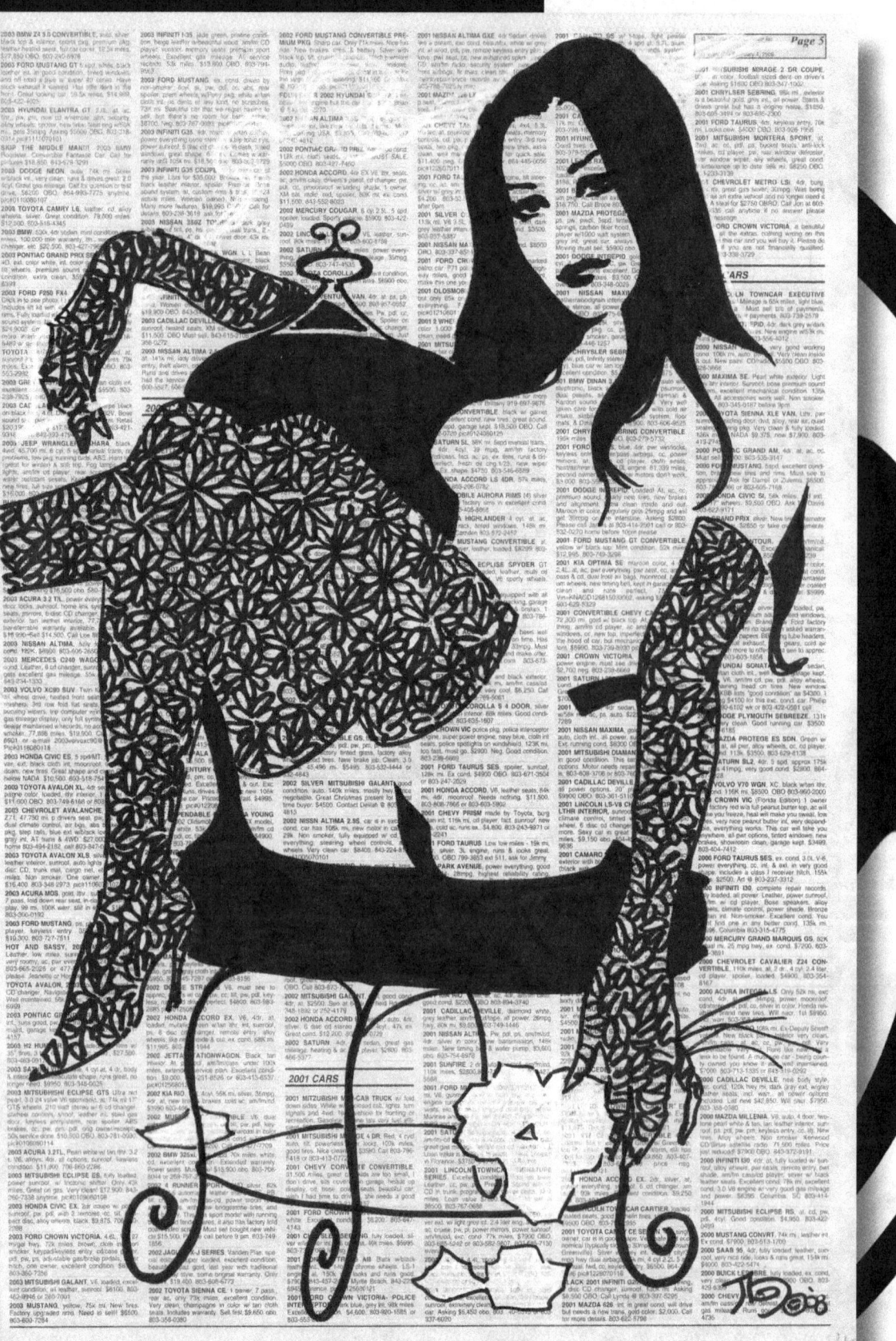

NUMBER 40 Frieda Never Learns

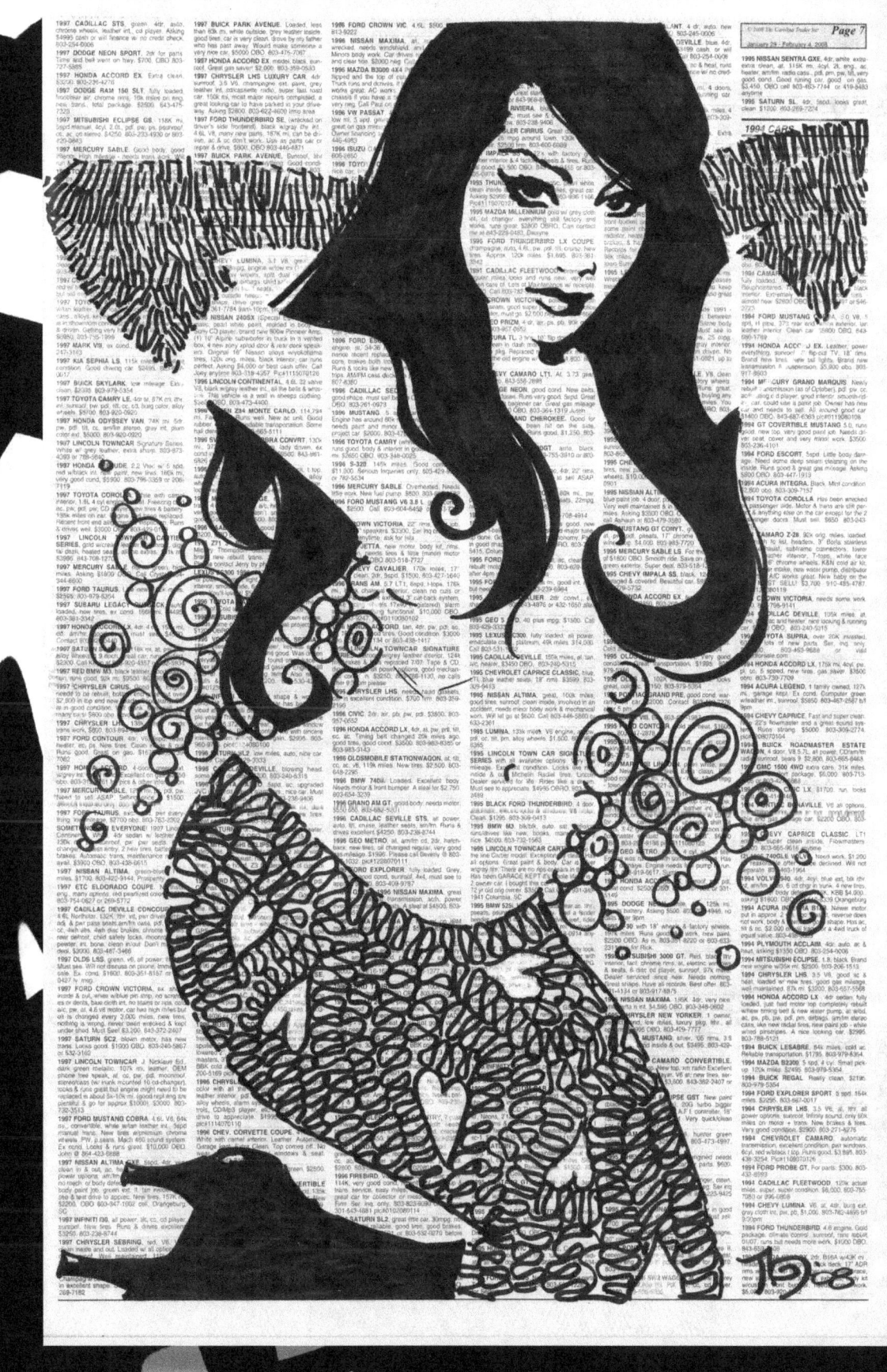

NUMBER 41

UP MY Sleeve

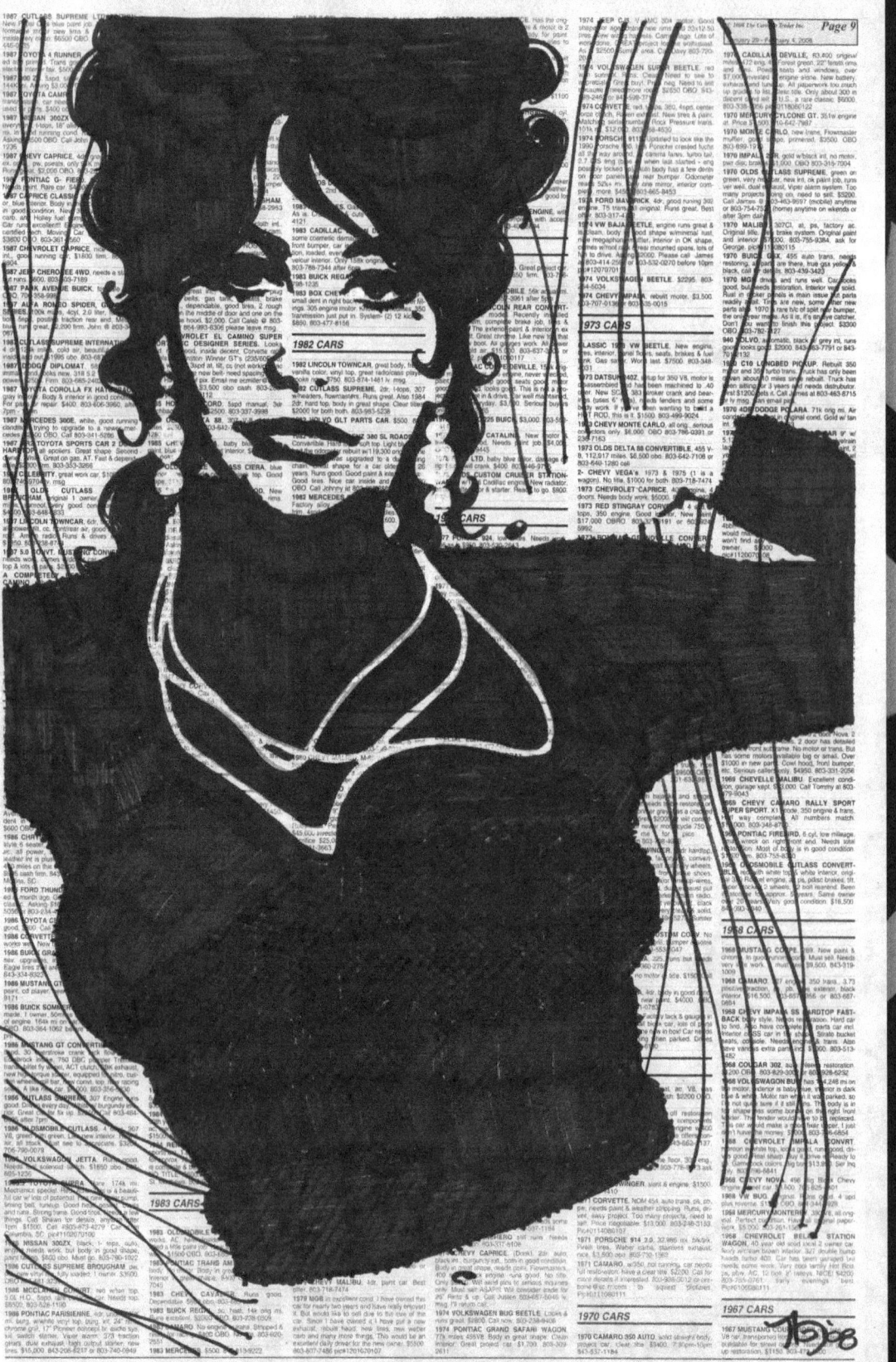

NUMBER 42   Draw Me a Map

NUMBER 43

I Left a Map

NUMBER 44 It Really Satisfies

NUMBER45 In The Pocket

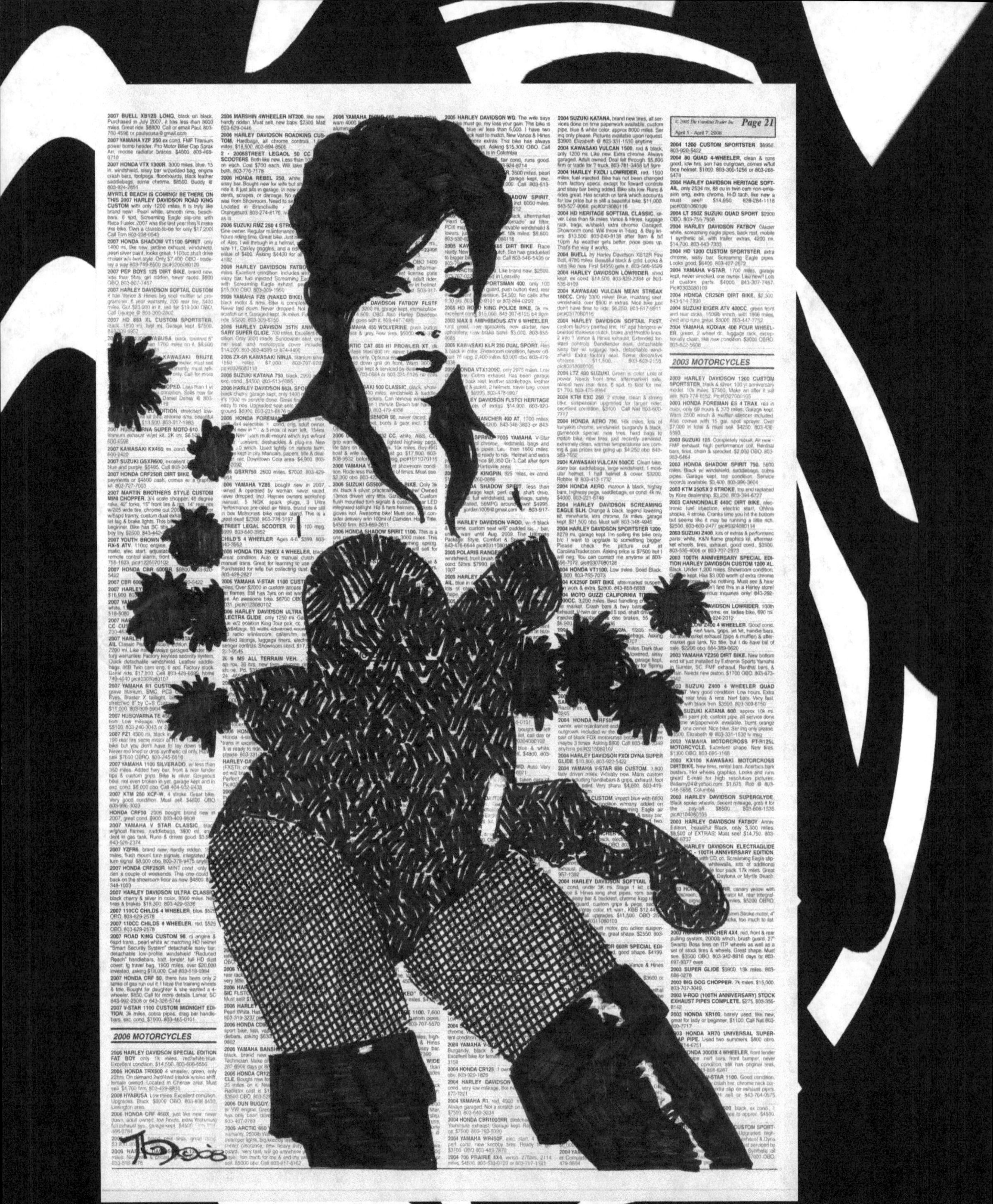
Page 21
2003 MOTORCYCLES
2006 MOTORCYCLES

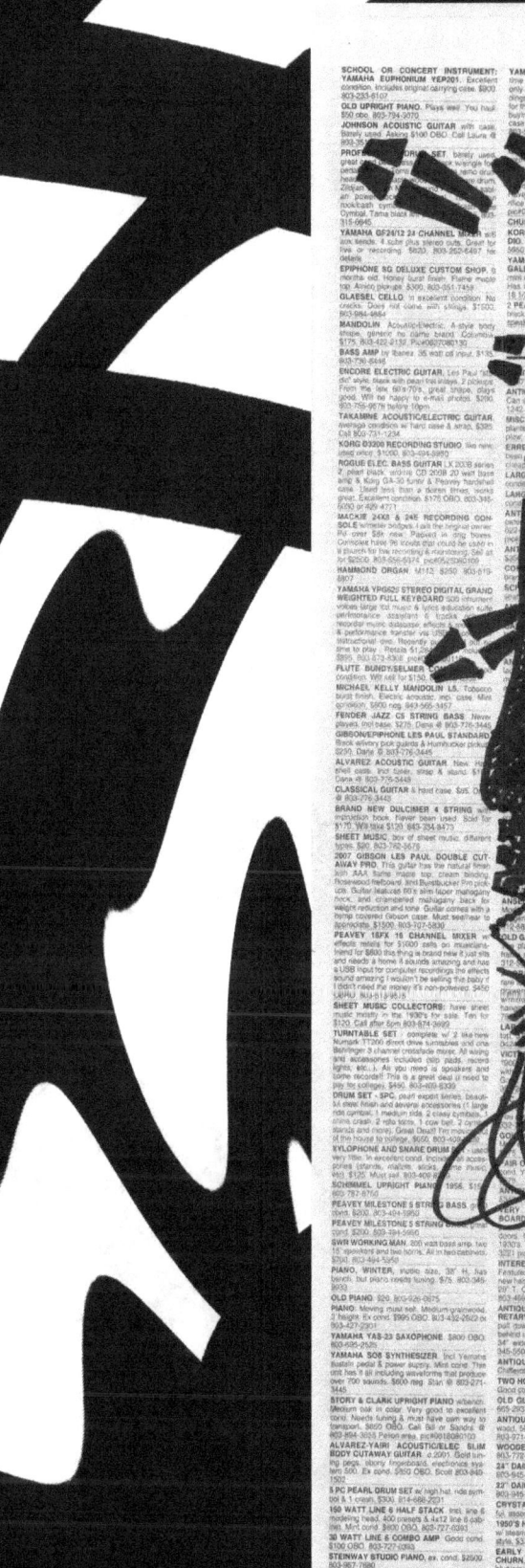

NUMBER 47 My Kozy Koffins

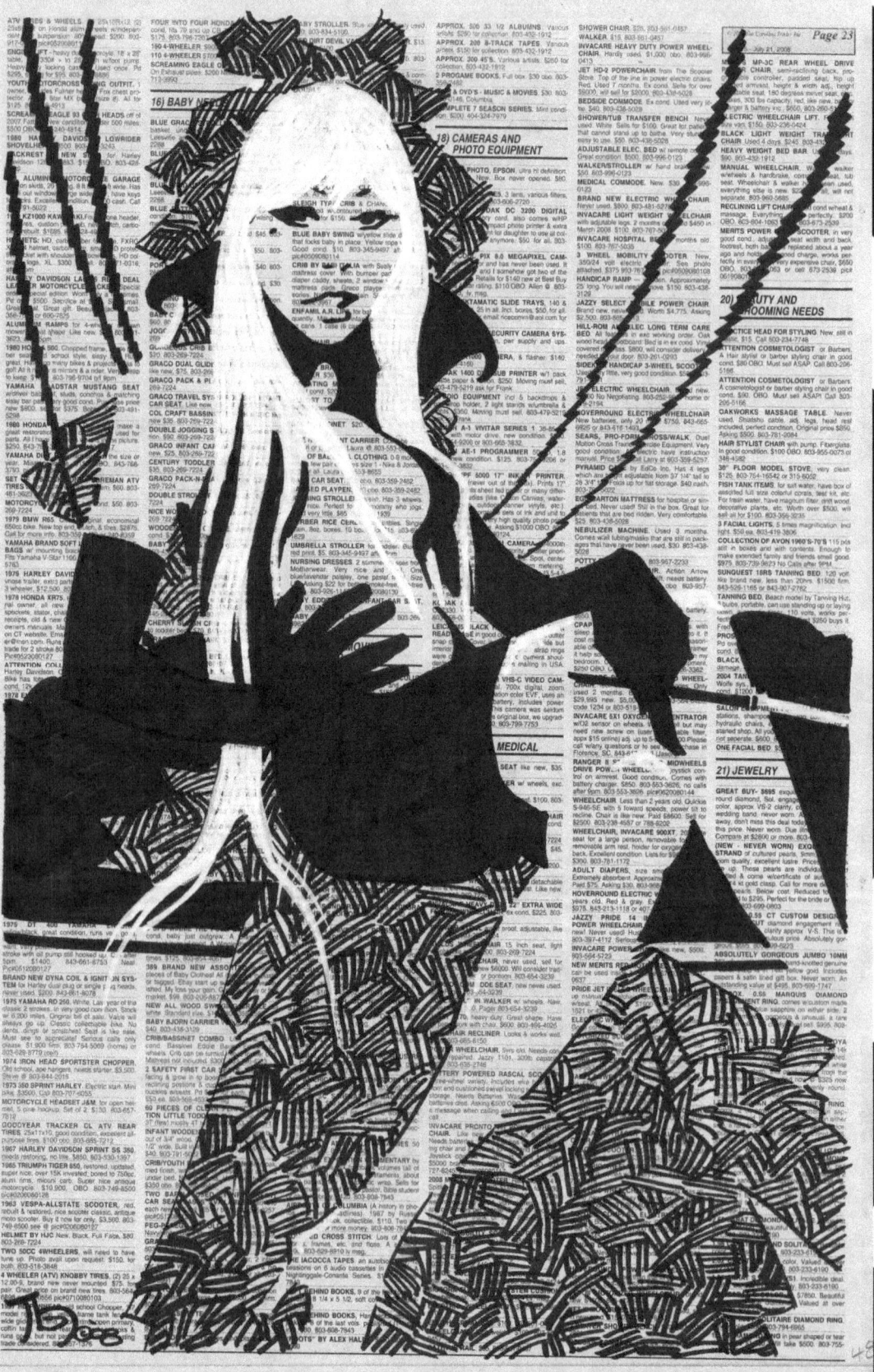

NUMBER 48 Boots are for Waltzing

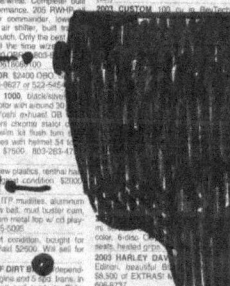

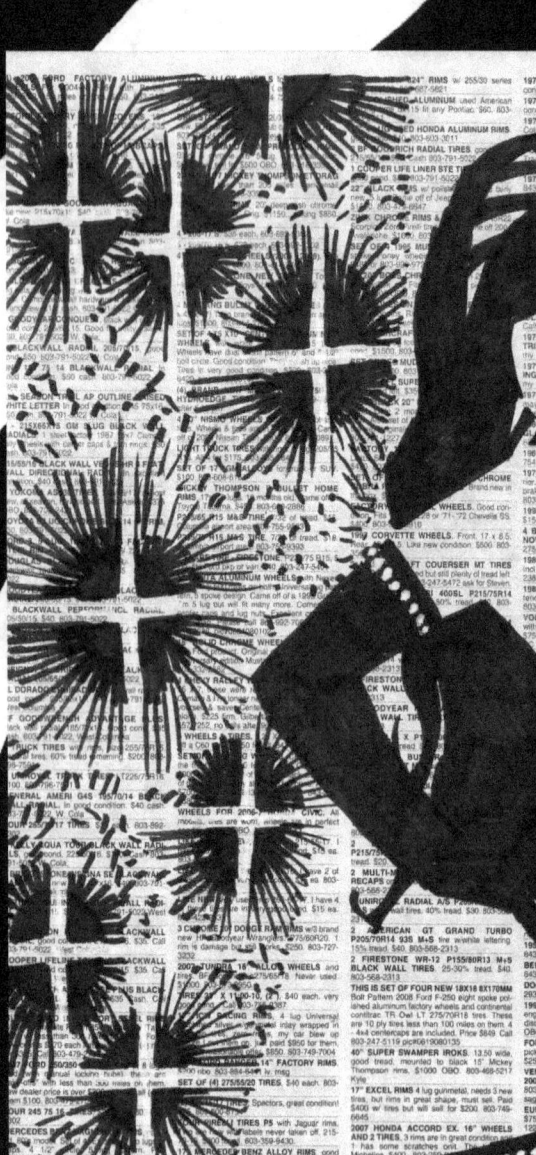

NUMBER50 You Gave Me a Tie

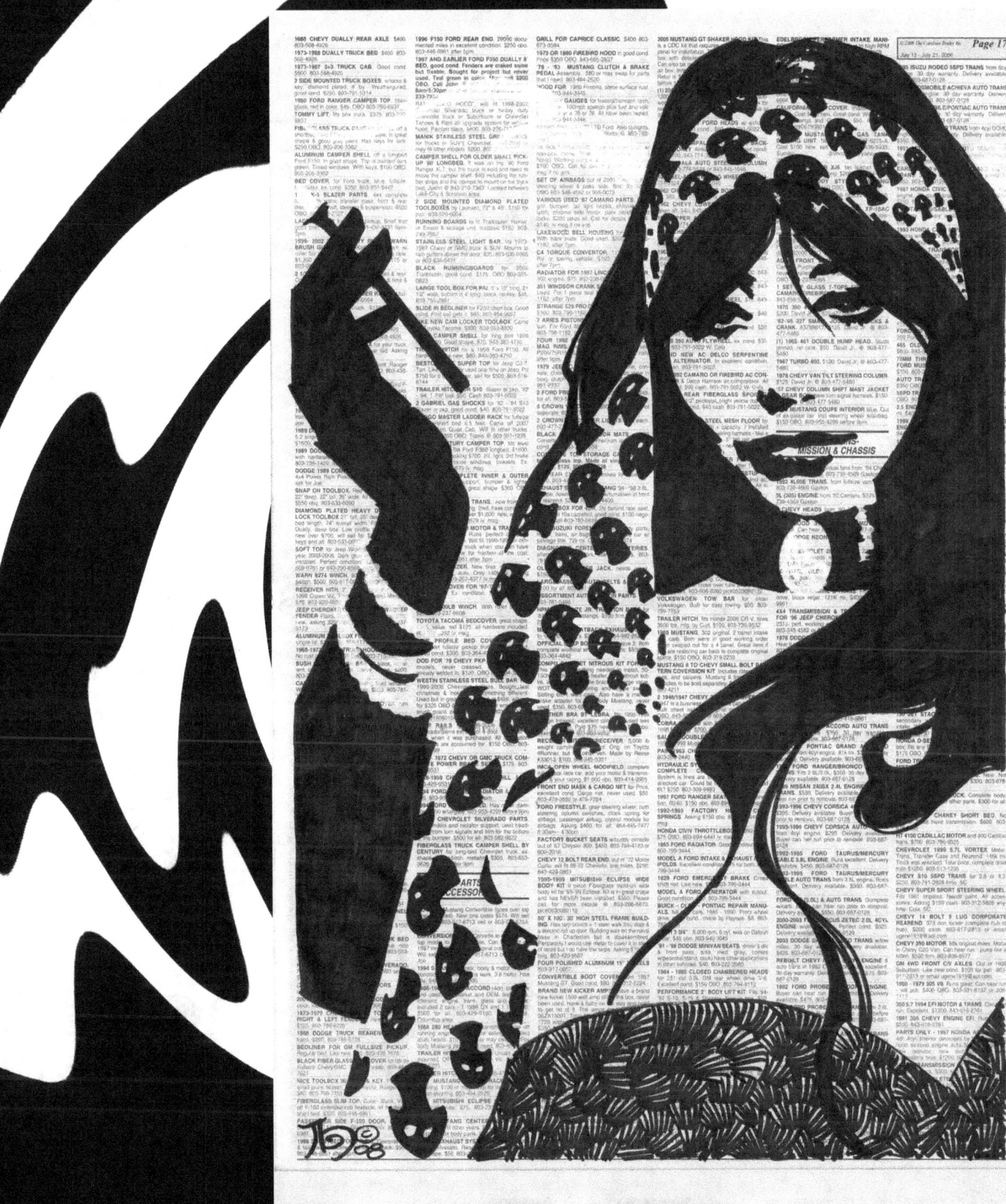

NUMBER 51 My Hippie Wedding

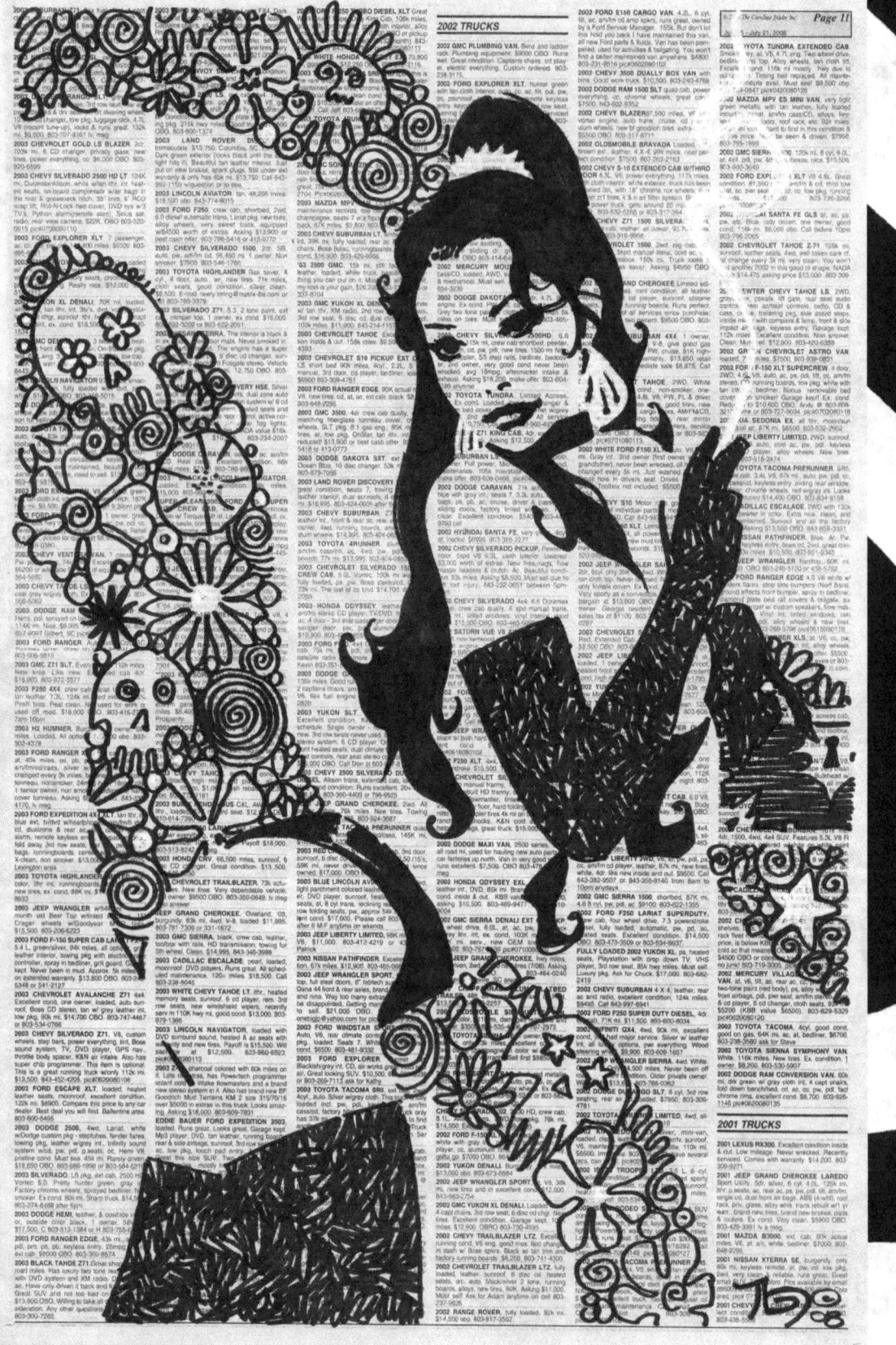

NUMBER 52) Her Candy Castle